*Oxford
Secondary
English*

Dimensions

Book 3

John Seely
Frank Green
Graham Nutbrown

Oxford University Press   1988

Oxford University Press, Walton Street, Oxford OX2 6DP

Oxford New York Toronto
Delhi Bombay Calcutta Madras Karachi
Petaling Jaya Singapore Hong Kong Tokyo
Nairobi Dar es Salaam Cape Town
Melbourne Auckland

and associated companies in
Berlin Ibadan

Oxford is a trade mark of Oxford University Press

© Oxford University Press 1988
First published 1988

ISBN 0 19 833170 3

Phototypeset by Best-set Typesetter Ltd., Hong Kong
Printed in Hong Kong

Contents

Unit one: Crime and punishment 4
Special A: Explosion 18

Unit two: You can't print that! 26
Special B: Advertising 38

Unit three: What's the problem? 44
Special C: Charity appeal 56

Unit four: Changing places 60
Special D: Journey to Asfodelia 76

Unit five: Life-style 84

Unit six: Where am I going? 96
Special E: Summer holiday job 108

Reference section 114
Planning and drafting 114
Letters 118
Punctuation 122
Word study 126
Acknowledgements 128

Crime and punishment

Questions

1   Why has the youth leader done this?
2   Is there anything else she could have done?
3   What would you have done if you were the youth leader?
4   What is your opinion of the leader's action?

Questions

1 Why has he been taken to the police station?
2 What do you think will happen to him?
3 What do you think of the way he has behaved?
4 What do you think of the way he has been treated?
5 What would each of these people think of the way he has been treated?

    the boy   the police
    his parents the youth leader

Writing

Copy and complete each of these statements of opinion. Explain fully what each person thinks and feels about what has happened.

1 'I'm the boy's mother. When I heard what had happened...'
2 'I'm the boy. I went back for my jacket. What I think is...'
3 'I'm the policeman who was on duty at the time. It seems to me that...'
4 'As the youth leader I have a responsibility to protect the Centre. This boy...'

Punishment

When someone is found guilty of breaking the law, or even the school rules, we expect them to be punished. But why?

Which of the opinions on this page do you think is right, and why?

It's to deter them. If people know they'll be punished, it makes them think twice before doing something wrong.

It's to show people that we don't like the laws being broken. Punishment is our way of saying, 'Breaking the law is wrong and we disapprove of crime,' so criminals are punished.

It serves them right. What's the point in the rest of us obeying the laws if people who break them get away with it? Punishment is our way of getting our own back on people who do wrong.

How?

People in different countries and living at different times have had widely-varying ideas about how criminals should be punished. Take sheep-stealing for example. Different societies have had the following penalties for sheep-stealing:

> execution
> transportation (from England to Australia)
> chopping off the right hand
> imprisonment
> fines
> probation

Why have different societies punished the same crime in such a variety of ways?

It's to put other people off. If they see someone being punished for a crime, then they'll think twice before trying it themselves.

What's the point of prison?

In Britain serious crimes are punished by imprisonment. People have different ideas about **why** criminals are locked up in prison. Which of these do you agree with, and why?

It's to keep them out of the way of ordinary decent people for a while – it's to protect us.

It should be as unpleasant as possible. They aren't supposed to enjoy it. They should hate it so much that they never want to go back into prison again.

Just taking away a person's liberty is a big punishment. Prisoners can never do what they want to. They always have to do what someone else says. Imprisonment is the punishment – you don't have to make it dirty and uncomfortable as well.

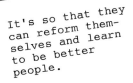

It's so that they can reform themselves and learn to be better people.

Kinds of punishment

These are some of the kinds of punishment which can be given to people convicted of crime:

probation	community service order
local prison	youth detention centre
open prison	high security prison

1. Make sure that you know what each of these means.
2. For each one make a list of advantages and disadvantages to:
   a) the court
   b) society
   c) the person sentenced.
3. Can you think of other punishments that would be suitable for particular crimes?

7

For and against

Grimshaws is a large department store in the middle of town. They have had a lot of shop-lifting recently, so the Manager has decided that all the staff must be very strict about all cases of shop-lifting.

Mandy Rees was in Grimshaws with a friend. For a dare she took a nylon scarf and walked out of the shop without paying for it. One of the assistants caught her and the store decided to prosecute.

At the magistrates' court, Mandy admitted taking the scarf. The magistrates have to decide what to do with her. Should they:

a) Let her off with a warning?
b) Fine her?
c) Put her on probation for six months?
d) Impose some other punishment? Think of a suitable punishment.

Penalty	Reasons for	Reasons against
Let her off with a warning		
Fine her		
Probation		
My idea:		
My idea:		

Looking at the possibilities

To help you make up your mind, copy out this table and then fill in the spaces with as many ideas as you can.

Making up your mind

Look at the ideas you have written down. Think about each one. Decide which you think is most suitable for Mandy **and** satisfactory for Grimshaws.

Arguing your case

Now decide what is the best way to argue your case. You need to do these things:

a) State which action it is best for the magistrates to take.
b) Give your reasons for thinking this is best.
c) Explain why you think the others are not suitable.

Passing sentence

Now it's your turn to be the judge. In each of the cases that follows, the jury has found the accused guilty of the crime. You have to pass sentence. A number of possible punishments are listed after each crime. You can choose one of these. You may think that none is suitable and, in this case, try and think of a better solution yourself. Whatever you do, you must give your reasons, as you did in the case of Mandy.

Malicious damage: Part one

Two boys found a car left by the edge of a disused quarry. It had apparently been abandoned. They broke into it, released the handbrake and pushed it over the edge into the quarry. A policeman happened to see them and arrested them for malicious damage to private property. Although the car had been abandoned, it was still the property of the person who had left it there.

Penalties:
   One year's probation
   25 days' community service, helping clear up the quarry
   Youth custody for three months
   Absolute discharge (no punishment)

Malicious damage: Part two

Dr Bright works in a busy city practice. He does a lot of emergency work for which he needs his car. One night, when he was on duty, two teenage girls broke into his car, released the handbrake and pushed it down a steep hill so that it smashed into a building at the bottom. When Dr Bright hurried out to go to an emergency, he found his car smashed up at the bottom of the hill. He was unable to attend the patient, who later died. She might have lived if he had got to her in time.

Penalties:
   One year's probation
   25 days' community service, helping the doctor
   Youth custody for three months
   Absolute discharge

The tropical fish con

This is a story about a confidence trickster called Les. It has been divided into seven sections. The first section, A, has been printed at the start, but the others have been jumbled up. Read them carefully and work out the correct order.

A It started out as a proper business project. Someone had invented an aquarium. It was for the entrance halls of business and office buildings. It was very large and it contained special feeding and cleaning equipment so that it only had to be serviced every two months.

B Les would then get very stroppy indeed. 'Don't be silly,' he'd go. 'Don't be so ignorant. What you've got there are **very young** tropical fish. They develop all their colours as they get older.'

C Les was undeterred. Round he went to offices, banks and estate agents and cheerfully signed up a long list of eager punters. And into foyers and reception areas went the magnificent tanks. They were stocked to the brim, not with brightly-coloured sword-tails, platys, tetras, loaches and plecs, but with what Les affectionately called 'little black and grey beggars' who could live anywhere.

D Not surprisingly, the phone started to ring after a couple of weeks.
   'Ah. Excuse me. I'm so sorry to bother you. But it's about the aquarium.'
   'That's a very good aquarium.'
   'Yes, yes. I'm certain it is. In fact, no complaints on that score. But it's just the fish.'

E What could be more attractive? Admittedly the hire fee was rather high – £200 a month. On the other hand customers and visitors were guaranteed the permanent sight of multicoloured tropical fish swimming contentedly around their self-sufficient tank.

F 'Yes?'
   'Well, I thought you said we'd be getting tropical fish.'
   'Yes.'
   'Well, the ones we've got seem to be all black and grey.'

G There was only one snag. The tanks did deliver the right amount of food at the right time, and the filter system really did keep them clean. Unfortunately the water wasn't kept warm enough for your actual tropical fish to survive.

adapted from *In the Underworld*
by **Laurie Taylor**

What happens next?

Write a continuation of the story. It might be about one of the owners of these 'young tropical fish', or it might be about the next bright idea thought up by Les.

Find the clues

Detective Inspector Hawkeye is investigating a robbery. He suspects a well-known thief, Harry 'the fingers' Crump. This is what happens when he visits him.

The evening gift

He had a most curious occupation in life. Having failed in every effort, he had to accept it with gratitude and enthusiasm; he received thirty rupees a month for it. He lived on fifteen rupees in a cheap hotel, where he was given a sort of bunk in the loft, with rafters touching his head. He saved fifteen rupees for paying off the family loan in the village incurred over his sister's marriage. He added a rupee or two to his income by filling money order forms and postcards for unlettered villagers, whom he met on the post office veranda. But his main work was very odd. His business consisted in keeping a wealthy drunkard company. This wealthy man wanted someone to check his drink after nine in the evening and take him home. Sankar's physique qualified him for this task. 'Don't hesitate to use force on me if necessary,' his employer had told him. But that was never done. Sankar did all that he could by persuasion and it was a quite familiar sight at the Oriental Café Bar – the wrangling going on between the employer and his servant. But Sankar with a margin of five minutes always succeeded in wresting the gentleman from his cups and pushing him into his car. On the following morning he was asked: 'What time did we reach home last night?'

'Nine-fifteen, sir –'

'Did you have much trouble?'

'No, sir –'

'Nine-fifteen! – very good, very good. I'm glad. On no account should you let me stay on beyond nine, even if I am in company –'

'Yes, sir.'

'You may go now, and be sure to be back in the evening in time –'

That finished his morning duty. He went back to his garret, slept part of the day, loitered about post offices, courts, etc., and returned to work at six o'clock.

'Come on,' said his employer, who waited for him on the veranda, and Sankar got into the front seat of the car and they drove off to the Oriental Café.

Today he was in a depressed state, he felt sick of his profession, the perpetual cajoling and bullying, the company of a drunkard. He nearly made up his mind to throw up this work and go back to the village. A nostalgia for his home and people seized him. 'I don't care what happens, I will get back home and do something else to earn this money.' On top of this mood came a letter from home: 'Send a hundred rupees immediately. Last date for mortgage instalment. Otherwise we shall lose our house –' He was appalled! Where could he find the money? What was

the way out? He cursed his lot more than ever. He sat for a long
time thinking of a way out. 'Our good old home! – Let it go if
it is to go.' It was their last possession in this world. If it went,
his mother, brothers, and his little sister would have to wander
about without a roof over their heads. But could he find a hundred
rupees? What did they mean by putting it off till the last moment?
He cursed his lot for being the eldest son of a troubled family.

He swung into duty as usual. He held the curtain apart for his
master as he entered the cubicle. He pressed a bell. He might be a
machine, doing this thing for thirty days in the month for nearly
twelve months now. The waiter appeared. No talk was necessary.
Sankar nodded. The waiter went away and returned a few
minutes later with an unopened flat bottle, a soda, and a glass
tumbler; he placed these on the table and withdrew.

'Bring this master a lemon squash,' the gentleman said.

'No, sir –' Sankar would reply; this ritual was repeated every
day. Now Sankar's business would be to pour out a measure of
drink into the tumbler, push it up, and place the soda near at
hand, go out on to the veranda, and read a newspaper there
(with the flat bottle in his pocket), and stay there till he was
called in again to fill the glass. By about ten to nine the last ounce
of drink would be poured out, and Sankar would sit down
opposite his master instead of going out to the veranda. This was
a sort of warning bell.

'Why do you sit here? Go to the veranda.'

'I like this place, sir, and I will sit here.'

'It is not time for you to come in yet.'

'Just ten minutes more, sir.'

'Nonsense. It is just seven o'clock.'

'About two hours ago –'

'You people seem to turn up the clock just as you like – let me see how much is left in the bottle –'

'Nothing,' Sankar said, holding up the bottle. 'The last drop was poured out.' He held up the bottle and the other became furious at the sight of it.

'I think,' he said with deep suspicion, 'there is some underhand transaction going on – I don't know what you have been doing on the veranda with the bottle –' Sankar learnt not to answer these charges. As the clock struck nine, he tapped the other's shoulder and said, 'Please finish your drink and get up, sir –'

'What do you mean by it? I'm not getting up. Who are you to order me?' Sankar had to be firm.

'Look here, don't you be a fool and imagine I am talking in drink. I am dead sober – leave me alone –'

Sankar persisted.

'I dismiss you today, you are no longer in my service. I don't want a disobedient fool for a companion, get out –' Usually Sankar sat through it without replying, and when the drink was finished he gently pulled the other up and led the way to the car, and the other followed, scowling at him with red eyes and abusing him wildly. Today when his employer said, 'I dismiss you, get out this minute –'

Sankar replied, 'How can you dismiss me all of a sudden! Must I starve?'

'No. I will give you four months' salary if you get out this moment.' Sankar thought it over.

'Don't sit there. Make up your mind quickly,' said his master. One hundred and twenty rupees! Twenty rupees more than the debt. He could leave for his village and give the cash personally to his mother, and leave his future to God. He brushed aside this vision, shook his head, and said: 'No, sir. You have got to get up now, sir.'

'Get out of my service –' shouted his master. He rang the bell and shouted for the waiter: 'Get me another –' Sankar protested to the waiter. 'Get out of here –' cried his master. 'You think I'm speaking in drink. I don't want you. I can look after myself. If you don't leave me, I will tell the waiter to neck you out –' Sankar stood baffled. 'Now young man –' He took out his wallet: 'What is your salary?'

'Thirty rupees, sir.'

'Here's your four months. Take it and be off. I have some

business meeting here, and I will go home just when I like, there
is the car.' He held out a hundred-rupee note and two tens.
Mortgage instalment. How can I take it? A conflict raged in
Sankar's mind, and he finally took the money and said: 'Thank
you very much, sir.'

'Don't mention it.'

'You are very kind.'

'Just ordinary duty, that is all. My principle is "Do unto others
as you would be done by others". You need not come in the
morning. I've no need for you. I had you only as a temporary
arrangement – I'll put in a word for you if any friend wants a
clerk or something of the sort –'

'Goodbye, sir.'

'Goodbye.' He was gone. The gentleman looked after him with
satisfaction, muttering: 'My principle is...unto others....'

Next morning Sankar went out shopping, purchased bits of
silk for his younger sister, a pair of spectacles for his mother, and
a few painted tin toys for the child at home. He went to the
hotel, looked into the accounts, and settled his month's bill. 'I'm
leaving today,' he said. 'I am returning to my village....' His
heart was all aflame with joy. He paid a rupee to the servant as a
tip. He packed up his trunk and bed, took a last look round his
garret; he had an unaccountable feeling of sadness at leaving the
familiar smoke-stained cell. He was at the bus stand at about
eleven in the day. The bus was ready to start. He took his seat.
He would be at home at six in the evening. What a surprise for his
mother! He would chat all night and tell them about the drunkard....

He was shaken out of this reverie. A police inspector standing at the footboard of the bus touched his shoulder and asked:

'Are you Sankar?'

'Yes.'

'Get down and follow me.'

'I am going to my village. . . .'

'You can't go now.' The inspector placed the trunk and bed on a coolie's head and they marched to the police station. There Sankar was subjected to much questioning, and his pockets were searched and all his money was taken away by the inspector. The inspector scrutinised the hundred-rupee note and remarked: 'Same number. How did you get this? Be truthful. . . .'

Presently the inspector got up and said: 'Follow me to the gentleman's house. . . .' Sankar found his employer sitting in a chair on the veranda, with a very tired look on his face. He motioned the inspector to a chair and addressed Sankar in a voice full of sorrow. 'I never knew you were this sort, Sankar. You robbed me when I was not aware of it. If you'd asked me I'd have given you any amount you wanted. Did you have to tie me up and throw me down?' He showed the bruises on his arm. 'In addition to robbing?' Sankar stood aghast. He could hardly speak for trembling. He explained all that had happened in the evening. His master and the police inspector listened in grim silence with obvious scepticism. His master said to the inspector: 'Can you believe anything of what he says?'

'No, sir,' replied the inspector.

'Nor can I. The poor fellow is driven to a corner and is inventing things....' He thought for a moment. 'I don't know ...I think...since you have recovered the amount...how much did you find with him?'

'About one hundred and ten rupees and some change...' said the inspector.

'What happened to the balance?' He turned to Sankar and asked:

'Did you spend it?'

'Yes, I bought some toys and clothes....'

'Well, well,' said the gentleman with a flourish. 'Let it go, poor devil: I'm sorry for you. You could have asked me for money instead of robbing me by force. Do you know where they found me?' he asked, showing the bruises on his elbow. 'Do you know it was nearly next day they took me home? You'd left me unconscious: I will, however, withdraw the complaint. "Do unto others as you would be done by" is my motto. You have served me faithfully all these months...but don't come before me again, you are a rogue. Get away now....'

'Inspector, after the formalities are over you may send me the seized amount tomorrow, thank you very much....'

Sankar starved for two days, and wandered about the street without a place for his head or trunk. At last, loitering near the post office one day, he had a few money orders and postcards to write, which earned him a rupee. With it he ate a meal, and took the bus for his village and back to all the ancient never-ending troubles of his family life.

R.K. Narayan

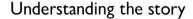

Understanding the story

1   Explain what Sankar's job was and how he did it.
2   On the day the story starts he was fed up. Why?
3   How did that evening with the rich gentleman differ from previous evenings?
4   Why was Sankar arrested?
5   How does the story end?

Thinking about the story

What is your opinion of
a) Sankar's behaviour
b) the rich gentleman's behaviour?

Explosion

Explosion may have been terrorist bomb

THREE PEOPLE were killed in the explosion at the Europa Cinema in the centre of Hinchester yesterday evening. Dozens more were taken to hospital, some with severe injuries.

The cause of the explosion is not yet known, but police are investigating reports that

Police have now appealed for anyone who

Police and army experts are now sorting through the rubble to find out exactly what

Eye witnesses described the chaos and horror as hundreds of people leaving the cinema at 10.15 were

The Chief Constable, Mr Alfred Downton, said early this morning that the public can rest assured that the police will not cease their investigations until

Emergency services were on the spot within minutes. Members of the public joined them as they tried to

(Further reports and interviews on page 7)

The reporter's story

Imagine that you are the newspaper reporter who arrived at the scene of the explosion.

1   Copy and complete the newspaper report, by filling in the gaps.
2   It says that there are 'further reports and interviews on page 7' of the newspaper. Think about who the reporter might have spoken to. Write a report of one of these interviews.

Susan Baker's story: Part one

Susan Baker is eighteen. She left school last year and now works as a sales assistant in a sports shop. On the night of November 8th she was in the centre of Hinchester with her boy-friend Matthew Coleman. They had been to a disco at the Top Deck Club and at 10.20 pm were on their way to the bus-stop near the Prince Albert Hotel.

Suddenly the crowd leaving the Europa Cinema started running and screaming. At the same time Susan was staggered by the blast of an explosion. Flying glass and debris scattered all around her. She was immediately aware that Matthew had collapsed to the ground.

The danger seemed over in a flash, but people continued to rush around her, many screaming from the pain of their injuries. Others, including Matthew, lay unconscious on the ground. As the wailing ambulances arrived, Matthew regained consciousness, but he was obviously severely injured.

Susan went with Matthew in the ambulance. She was startled to hear him repeating over and over again, 'Why didn't Tony stop? He saw me, I know he did!'

In a flash Susan remembered seeing Matthew's brother, Tony Coleman, in the crowd running away from the cinema. She also recalled some recent gossip about Tony being mixed up with a sinister group known as DAG (Direct Action Group) at his college. Susan couldn't understand why Tony had not stopped to help his brother.

Imagine that you are Susan. You wait for the ambulance and then travel in it to the hospital with Matthew. Describe what you can see and hear, and your thoughts and feelings.

The Nurse's story

Mary Hewitt, a 19-year-old student nurse, had just come on duty at Hinchester Royal Hospital, when the first news of the explosion came through. While ambulances rushed to the scene, Mary and the other hospital staff prepared for what turned out to be one of the busiest nights of their lives.

1 What preparations would they have made?
2 Write down Mary's thoughts and feelings as she got ready for the first casualties to arrive.

Mary was soon busy helping to wheel casualties into the hospital from the ambulance. She had to comfort and reassure the victims **and** their friends and relations. Some of the victims were severely injured; others were suffering from shock.

1 Make a list of the skills and personal qualities Mary would need to cope with this situation.
2 How would **you** have coped? Explain your answer.

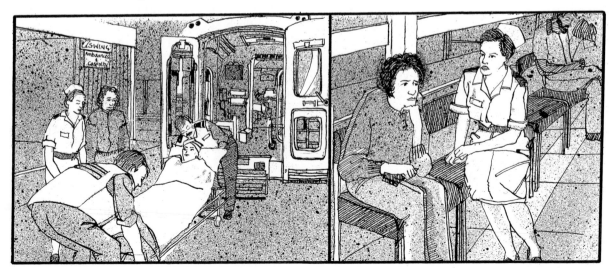

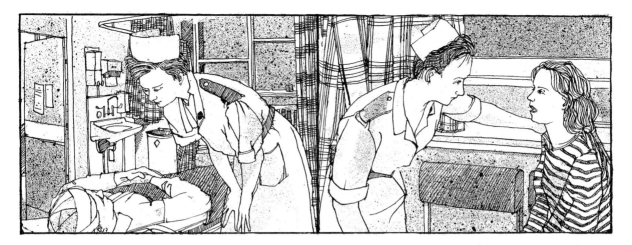

One of the victims Mary was most involved with was Matthew Coleman. Matthew was delirious, still murmuring about his brother Tony. Mary was puzzled and curious: she had known Tony at school and liked him.

Matthew had an emergency operation to remove splinters of glass from his body. While Susan waited anxiously, Mary asked her what Matthew had meant about Tony. Susan was so upset and shocked at the time that she revealed rather more than she intended.

1 Write the conversation between Mary and Susan.
2 The next day, when she has come off duty and had some rest, Mary writes about the previous night in her diary. What does she write?

Susan Baker's story: Part two

As she left the hospital in the early hours of the morning, having waited to make sure that Matthew was off the danger list, a number of thoughts were going through Susan's mind. What had caused the explosion? Was it a bomb? Had Tony seen Matthew? If so, why hadn't he stopped? Could Tony be involved in terrorism?

Susan knew she had to find some answers. She had to do something. But what?

1 Make notes of the alternative courses of action Susan could take.
2 What extra information does she need to find out?
3 Make a timetable for how Susan will spend the next 24 hours.

Remember Susan's main loyalty is to Matthew. For his sake she must discover the truth about what happened.

Tony Coleman's story

Anthony James COLEMAN

Date of birth: 21/7/68
Last known address:
  17, Portview Avenue, Hinchester
Height: 1.81m
Build: stocky
Hair: dark brown
Eyes: brown/wears glasses occasionally
Other features: mole on left cheek

At present Anthony Coleman is a 3rd-year student at Hinchester College, studying Economics. He is known to have taken part in demonstrations organised by the Direct Action Group. There is no evidence that he has ever been a full member of the Group. In his second year at college he shared a flat with Kevin Pople and Thomas Slater, both known active members of DAG. (Files available on both) Coleman now lives alone in a bedsit. He appears to be a hardworking student. He has never been convicted or suspected of any criminal activity.

9th November, 11.15 hours

Statement by ANTHONY JAMES COLEMAN

On the afternoon of Saturday November 8th I was working in my room when I received a phone call from Tom Slater. I used to share a flat with him and Kevin Pople, but I moved out when they started to put pressure on me to join them in what I considered to be extremist activities on behalf of DAG. I did sympathise with their views to some extent, but their plans for direct action were becoming more and more aggressive and I just didn't want to get involved. Tom had phoned me to ask me to meet him out-side the Europa Cinema at 10pm that evening. He said he was in some kind of trouble and he needed help. Reluctantly I agreed to help him. I still felt some friendship for him.

I arrived at the cinema about one minute after 10pm. When I had waited for fifteen minutes I began to walk away. Then I spotted Tom in the phone-box across the street. At the same moment a crowd of people swarmed out of the cinema and then there was an explosion. I got swept along with the crowd. I looked around for Tom, but he wasn't in the phone-box any more. About a hundred metres down the road I stopped to help an elderly man. I think he had had a heart attack. I stayed with him for a few minutes, until I heard the ambulances coming and then I slipped away.

I had been thinking that the explosion could have been the work of DAG and I didn't want to get involved. It was the kind of stupid action I had heard members of DAG discussing, but I never thought they would actually do it. I know I should have stayed to help more and to give a statement, but I just panicked. The next day, when I heard that my brother Matthew had been injured, I came to the police station to give this statement.

22

Detective Sergeant Richard Broome has the task of investigating Tony's case. Having read Tony's statement, he makes two lists:

a) Questions he wants to ask Tony.
b) Things he wants to check or find out about.

Then he begins to interview Tony.

1   Imagine that you are the Detective. Write down what you would put in your two lists.
2   Working with a partner, act out the interview between the Detective and Tony.
3   Now write the Detective's report on the interview.

23

The whole story

Susan's boyfriend Matthew was badly injured by the blast. . .

This is Jo Meadows reporting. At last it is possible to piece together exactly what happened in the terrifying bomb explosion at the Europa Cinema last week. Over the last week, I have been talking to people who were actually involved in the explosion. I began with Susan Baker. . .

I don't remember much about it, really. I was just walking towards the bus-stop when suddenly. . .

Matthew was taken to Hinchester Royal Hospital. Student Nurse Mary Hewitt recalled what happened next. . .

I was with my boyfriend, Matthew Coleman. We were on our way home from a disco when it happened. . .

We had about five minutes' warning that something terrible had happened. Then the ambulances started arriving. . .

But Susan Baker had noticed something very strange. She had seen Matthew's brother Tony running *away* from the scene of the explosion, even though she is sure that he had seen Matthew lying there injured. I eventually tracked down Tony Coleman. At first he wasn't keen to give me an interview, but eventually he agreed to. . .

Our enquiries began when Mr Coleman came to the station and made a statement. He told us. . .

It's all very complicated. You see I used to be friends with two students called Kevin Pople and. . .

It wasn't long before the police got on to the connection with Direct Action Group. Detective-Sergeant Broome takes up the story. . .

Finishing it off

What did each of the people say when they were interviewed? Look back through the work you have done and work out exactly what each one knew. Think about how each person would speak and describe the things that he or she had seen. Now build up the whole programme, by completing each interview. You can do this in a number of ways:

1 Group work
Each member of the group takes one of the characters and acts as that person.

2 Pair work
As a pair you do all the interviews, taking it in turns to be the interviewer.

3 Individual work
Make up part or all of the programme as a written script.

25

Questions

1 Describe how the reporter came to write the story.
2 Do you think that this is a common way of gathering news?
3 What do you think of the way the reporter behaved?
4 What else could he have done?

Slander and libel

In Norman times a slanderer not only had to pay damages, but also had to stand in the market-place, hold his nose between two fingers, and confess to being a liar. In the ninth century, Alfred the Great was not so lenient: persistent slanderers had their tongues cut out.

slander *n.* **1.** a false statement uttered maliciously that damages a person's reputation. **2.** the crime of uttering this. —*v.* to utter a slander about. —**slanderous** *adj.*, **slanderously** *adv.*

libel (**ly**-bĕl) *n.* **1.** a published false statement that damages a person's reputation. **2.** the act of publishing it, *was charged with libel.* **3.** (*informal*) a statement or anything that brings discredit on a person or thing, *the portrait is a libel on him.* —*v.* (libelled, libelling) to utter or publish a libel against. —**libellous** *adj.*

Questions

5 What is the main difference between slander and libel?
6 Was anybody in the story guilty of slander?
7 Was anybody in the story guilty of libel?
8 What would be a good modern punishment for slander and libel?

Writing

Using the headline in the picture, write the *Daily Splurge* story as you think it might have appeared.

Waitress at a conference

The following article appeared in the magazine of a school in the north of England.

Reporter: **Faith Blamires**

The annual conference of the NAS/UWT was held at the Spa during the holidays. I worked there as a waitress and cleared away after the meal was finished.

There were 1000 attenders – all teachers – who expected to be served at 11.10 for break and then left the used things to be collected. The mess they left took an hour and a half to clear away. They left packets, ashtrays, papers, pens, but not one tip all week.

But what was really shocking was the fact that teachers too can push and shove, shout and yell. I saw them knock over an elderly gentleman with an artificial leg, in their urgency to obtain a place in the queue. I saw many being discourteous, blocking the aisles that people had to walk down. Apart from that they were reasonably behaved.

However, when Sir Keith Joseph, the Secretary of State for Education, came on April 3rd, the teachers jeered at him and hurled shocking insults. When we act like this in school we are punished. Is this the example we have been set by teachers?

The article was published at a difficult time for teachers. For some months they had been taking industrial action. As a result they were being criticised by a number of people. Local teachers were quick to criticise the magazine article. The Deputy Head of the girl's school is reported to have said:

'As far as I'm concerned, this is just going to stir it up against teachers. It's mud-slinging.'

The Head of English, responsible for the magazine, is quoted as saying:

'The best thing I can do is to teach the value of using language to obtain the truth and present it fairly. Although this article hasn't made me popular, the story is factual, and no one can dispute it.'

The magazine article soon became a national issue. The local secretary of the teachers' union which had held the conference said that he had been in touch with the leadership of the union. They could find no evidence to support the 'so-called reporter's allegations'. He demanded an apology and a retraction from the school.

The Head of the school spoke about the girl reporter:

'I know her well. I have no reason to question her honesty and integrity.'
He said he could not apologise for the contents of the article, since the views expressed were the girl's observations. It was her perception of what she had seen. No one should forget that. He emphasised that the article was written by a fifteen year old:

'It was what she saw through her own eyes. If I'd been there I'd have doubtlessly viewed things differently, but I wasn't.' The Head did apologise for any trouble and embarrassment caused.

Understanding the arguments

1   Read the girl's article carefully. Write one or two sentences summing up her opinion of the behaviour of the teachers at the conference.
2   Make a list of the **facts** that led her to this opinion.
3   Read the rest of the page, looking for information about people who **criticised** the girl. Who were they?
4   Make a list of the reasons they gave.
5   Now look for information about people who **defended** the girl. Who were they?
6   Make a list of the reasons they gave.

Your opinion

Look at the work you have done so far. Think about your opinion. Remember that the people on **both** sides had good reasons for thinking that they were right. When you have thought about it, write down your opinion of what the girl did, and your reasons for it.

The article on the right has been submitted for the school magazine. Three people have to decide whether it should be published:
   The pupil who edits it
   The teacher in charge
   The Head.

1   Imagine that you are the pupil who edits the magazine. Would you want to publish the article? What would your reasons be?
2   If you were the teacher in charge would you allow it to be published? Why?
3   Suppose you were the Head. Would you want it to be published? What would your reasons be?

WHICH LESSON?

A Consumer's Guide to LESSONS and TEACHERS

For this report our reporters sampled the lessons of twenty teachers of the main subjects studied in the third and fourth years. We graded the lessons according to these standards:
* INTEREST
* HOW MUCH WE LEARNED
* HUMOUR
* VARIETY

A DISMAL PICTURE

We found a dismal picture. On the whole lessons were thought to be uninteresting, monotonous and lacking in humour. Only the classes taught by Mr Sinclair and Mrs Fredericks were thought to be interesting.

A BEST BUY

There's no doubt at all that Mr Sinclair's third year drama lessons are our best buy.

29

Getting them talking

Most stories contain some talking. When you are writing, it is sometimes difficult to know when to put in conversations and how much talking to have. Study these three versions of the same story.

A She found it quite easy to follow Langland off the ferry and on to the road out of St Malo. His red Elan was easy to spot, even when he got ahead of her on the open road. The trouble started when he reached a small village called La Chapelle. The Lotus suddenly pulled off the road in the main square and Langland switched the engine off and got out of the car. She had stopped just past him and was wondering what to do, when he strode towards her, wrenched open the car door and demanded to know what the hell she thought she was doing following him. She began by pretending innocence, but it soon became clear that he wasn't fooled. She decided that it was time she came out with her cover story. It had always been possible that he might realise she was following him, so she had invented a story about being a lifelong fan of his music, and wanting to find a chance to meet him. If she had hoped that this would convince him, she was sadly mistaken.

B She found it quite easy to follow Langland off the ferry and on to the road out of St Malo. His red Elan was easy to spot, even when he got ahead of her on the open road. The trouble started when he reached a small village called La Chapelle. The Lotus suddenly pulled off the road in the main square and Langland switched the engine off and got out of the car. She had stopped the car just past him and was wondering what to do, when he strode towards her and wrenched open the car door.

'What the hell do you think you're doing?' he demanded angrily.
'What do you mean?'
'Following me, that's what I mean.'
'No I'm not.'
'Where are you going, then?'
'I...er...South. Down to the South.'
'Where?'
'I haven't decided yet.'
'Precisely. That's just a cock-and-bull story and you know it.'
Maria thought fast. She decided that it was time she came out with her cover story. It had always been possible that he might realise she was following him, so she had invented a story about being a lifelong fan of his music, and wanting to find a chance to meet him. If she had hoped that this would convince him, she was sadly mistaken.

C Langland wrenched the car door open and leant in.

'What the hell do you think you're doing?' he demanded angrily.

'What do you mean?'

'Following me, that's what I mean.'

'No I'm not.'

'You've been on my tail since we got off the ferry. It must be easy enough following a car as distinctive as mine – it's the only red Lotus Elan I've seen on the road this morning.'

'I'm not following you, I tell you.'

'All right. Where are you going, then?'

'I . . . er . . . South. Down to the South.'

'Where?'

'I haven't decided yet.'

'Precisely. That's just a cock-and-bull story and you know it.'

'I suppose I'll have to tell you the truth, then.'

'It might be a good idea. Come on then, out with it.'

'I saw you on the ferry and recognised you. I've always been a fan of your music. I've got all the records, absolutely all of them.'

'That's what they all say.'

'But it's true. And as I hadn't decided where I was going in France – I'm camping and I can go where I like – I thought I'd follow you. Just for fun, to see what happened.'

'I don't believe a word of it.'

Thinking about the story

Read each of the three extracts carefully.

1 Which one do you find easiest to read and why?
2 Which is the most interesting and why?
3 Which is the hardest to read and why?
4 The three versions do not contain exactly the same information. In what ways does the information in them differ? Make a list of the main differences.

Narrative and dialogue

The technical term for story-telling is narrative. The technical term for conversation is dialogue. Version A is all narrative and no dialogue. Version B is a mixture of narrative and dialogue. Version C is almost entirely dialogue.

1 Which version is the most suitable for telling a story like this?
2 What are your reasons for thinking this version is the most suitable?
3 What kind of story do you think is most suited to the approach of version A?
4 What kind of story do you think is most suited to the approach of version B?

Scoop!

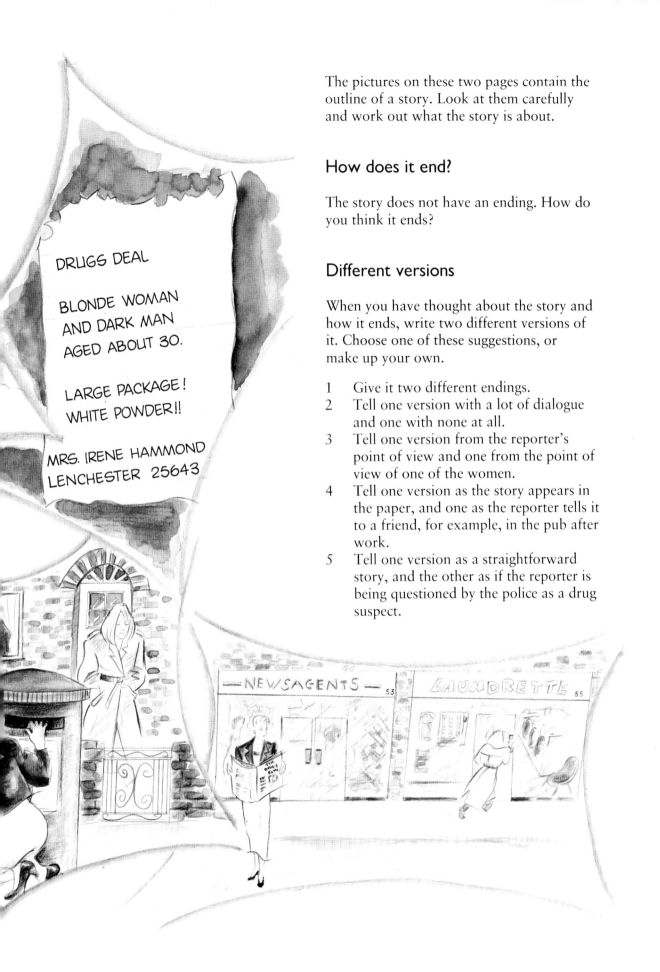

The pictures on these two pages contain the outline of a story. Look at them carefully and work out what the story is about.

How does it end?

The story does not have an ending. How do you think it ends?

Different versions

When you have thought about the story and how it ends, write two different versions of it. Choose one of these suggestions, or make up your own.

1   Give it two different endings.
2   Tell one version with a lot of dialogue and one with none at all.
3   Tell one version from the reporter's point of view and one from the point of view of one of the women.
4   Tell one version as the story appears in the paper, and one as the reporter tells it to a friend, for example, in the pub after work.
5   Tell one version as a straightforward story, and the other as if the reporter is being questioned by the police as a drug suspect.

DRUGS DEAL

BLONDE WOMAN AND DARK MAN AGED ABOUT 30.

LARGE PACKAGE! WHITE POWDER!!

MRS. IRENE HAMMOND LENCHESTER 25643

—NEWSAGENTS—   53

LAUNDRETTE   55

Headline news

Sometimes newspapers produce headlines and other statements that are very misleading. For each of the following, explain:

1   what it was probably about
2   what it **could** have been about
3   how it could be rewritten to make clear and correct sense.

SUPER TRAIN TALKS

British bird men held by Turkey

Filming in cemetery angers residents

THREE BATTERED IN FISH SHOP

Body in garden was plant says wife

Slippery fish make jam on M2

Traffic will hit homes if motorway is scrapped

YOUTH HIT BY TRAIN IS RUSHED TO TWO HOSPITALS

Injury forces Miss Truman to scratch

SPOTTED MAN WANTED FOR QUESTIONING

Foot in mouth

People can say silly things. These quotations come from television or radio programmes. For each one, say

1 in what circumstances it might have been said
2 what is silly about it
3 what the person ought to have said.

HE HAS WAITED 62 YEARS TO MEET THE BROTHER HE NEVER KNEW HE HAD.

"FIFTY-EIGHT PER CENT OF ALL CARS COMING INTO BRITAIN ARE IMPORTED."

"I OWE A LOT TO MY PARENTS, ESPECIALLY MY MOTHER AND FATHER."

Next week we'll be looking at the Tour de France – all those bicycles roaring through the countryside.

Conditions on the road are bad, so if you are just setting off for work, leave a little earlier.

"TRAFFIC IN THE WANDSWORTH ONE-WAY SYSTEM IS VERY HEAVY IN BOTH DIRECTIONS."

Football's a game of skill – we kicked them a bit and they kicked us a bit.

"AND THE SECOND GOAL WAS A BLUEPRINT OF THE FIRST."

IT'S OBVIOUS THESE RUSSIAN SWIMMERS ARE DETERMINED TO DO WELL ON AMERICAN SOIL.

35

Gutter press

News Editor: Peer Confesses,
Bishop Undresses,
Torso wrapped in Rug,
Girl Guide Throttled,
Baronet Bottled,
J.P. Goes to Jug.

But yesterday's story's
Old and hoary.
Never mind who got hurt.
No use grieving,
Let's get weaving.
What's the latest dirt?

Diplomat Spotted,
Scout Garotted,
Thigh Discovered in Bog,
Wrecks Off Barmouth,
Sex in Yarmouth,
Woman in Love with Dog,
Eminent Hostess Shoots Her Guests,
Harrogate Lovebird Builds Two Nests.

Cameraman: *Builds two nests?*
Shall I get a picture of the lovebird singing?
Shall I get a picture of her pretty little eggs?
Shall I get a picture of her babies?

News Editor: No!
Go and get a picture of her legs.

Beast Slays Beauty,
Priest Flays Cutie,
Cupboard Shows Tell-Tale Stain,
Mate Drugs Purser,
Dean Hugs Bursar,
Mayor Binds Wife With Chain,
Elderly Monkey Marries For Money,
Jilted Junky Says 'I Want My Honey'.

Cameraman: *Want my honey?*
Shall I get a picture of the pollen flying?
Shall I get a picture of the golden dust?
Shall I get a picture of the queen bee?

News Editor: No!
Go and get a picture of her bust.

Judge Gets Frisky,
Nun Drinks Whisky,
Baby Found Burnt in Cot,
Show Girl Beaten,
Duke Leaves Eton –

Cameraman: *Newspaperman Gets Shot!*
May all things clean
And fresh and green
Have mercy upon your soul,
Consider yourself paid
By the hole my bullet made –

News Editor: (*dying*) Come and get a picture of the hole.

Paul Dehn

Questions

1 What does the poem mean by **Gutter press**?
2 The first six lines sum up the kind of story such newspapers print. What have these stories in common?
3 The next six lines describe the attitude of the News Editor. How would you explain this in your own words?
4 How does the rest of the poem develop these ideas?
5 The poem was published in 1965. Is it still a fair comment on some newspapers?
6 Which newspapers today are like this?
7 Why do they publish stories like these?
8 Is there anything wrong with doing this?

Research project

1 Get two different newspapers for the same day:
   a) one of the kind described in the poem,
   b) one that is not like that.
2 Compare their front pages:
   a) What story does each one consider most important?
   b) What else is there on the front page of each one?
3 Compare the rest of the news in each one.
4 Compare the main sports stories in each one.
5 Write a short explanation of the main differences between the two papers.

Advertising

Information and persuasion

The main purposes of any advertising are to inform people about a product and to persuade them to buy it. How these two things are done depends a lot on the product and the form of advertising used.

RENAULT 5 TS
1982, 1400 twin choke, Taxed 12 months, MoT, metallic blue, v.g.c., economical car, 45 mpg
£2,000
Tel. Carterton 841687

THE RIO. FOR UNDER 5 GRANDE.

RENAULT BUILD A BETTER CAR

£4,795 to be exact.

For that we offer an excellent rate of exchange.

Namely a 956cc engine, digital stereo radio/cassette, exclusive upholstery and a rather natty set of wheel trims.

Even a sunhatch that lets you soak up a full 524 square inches of our fabulous British climate.

If you prefer, there's also the more powerful 5 speed 1108cc TL model.

Like the TC, it comes in either red or silver.*

And likewise it too will go 547 miles on one tankful.

Not, we admit down to Rio but certainly to a few of our own, shall we say more exotic resorts.

All of which makes the Renault 5 Rio worth every single penny.

In any currency.

RENAULT
5

What's yours called?

SPECIAL EDITION
RENAULT 5 RIO FROM £4,795

RENAULT recommend elf lubricants.

They've got Michael.

Where did it happen?

What do they want?

Questions

For each of the four advertisements, answer these questions:

1 Where would you expect to find it?
2 What leads you to think this?
3 How much information does the advertisement contain about the product?
4 In what ways does it try to persuade you to buy the product?
5 How effective do you think it is?

Research

Find examples of advertisements to fit these categories:

1 Local newspaper.
2 Magazine.
3 Local radio. You'll have to listen carefully, probably more than once, and write down the main points it makes.
4 An advert that contains a lot of information.
5 An advert that is very persuasive.

Making up an advert

Now it's your turn. Make up an advertisement for the product described below. You can design your advertisement to be suitable for magazine, radio, or TV.

Electric socks

Recent developments in sock technology mean that cold feet are a thing of the past. Tiny microcircuits woven into the socks are connected to a lightweight battery worn in a special holder on the belt, or in the pocket. The batteries are rechargeable and one charge will last 24 hours, keeping the wearer's feet warm all day.

The right image

When a new product is launched, it has to present the right **image**. It has to look and sound right, so that it appeals to the people who are likely to buy it.

To do this, the advertiser has to think about the prospective consumers, and their:

age · income
social background · interests.

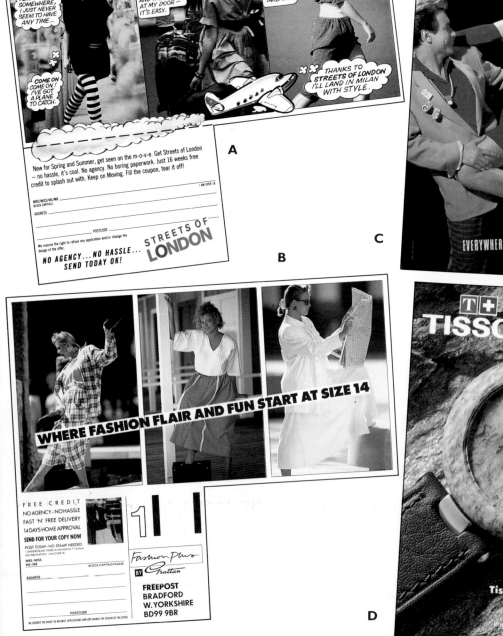

A

B

C

D

Questions

1   Adverts A and B are for mail order catalogues; they come from magazines read by different types of people. What kind of magazine do you think each comes from and why? In particular, think about their readers' age, social background, and income.

2   Adverts C and D come from the same magazine.
   a) What are the main differences between the pictures used?
   b) Pick out the key words in each advertisement.
   c) How would you describe the **image** of each product?
   d) What kind of person is each one aimed at?

Image and style

Sometimes advertisers try to give a product an image that is summed up in one picture, word or sound.

Questions

For each of the advertisements, answer these questions:

1   What is it advertising?
2   What does the image suggest to you?
3   Why has the advertiser chosen this image for this product?

41

Should it be allowed?

The essence of good advertising

The British Code of Advertising Practice says that all advertising must be:
- legal
- decent
- honest
- truthful
- responsible
- fair

Questions

1. Explain what you think each of these words means.
2. Can you think of ways in which advertisements might break each of these rules?

A code for children

The British Code of Advertising Practice contains special rules for particular kinds of advertisement. There are rules for adverts which contain children, or which are aimed at them. It says that adverts should not:

1. Try to persuade children to buy things unless they are things that they can afford.
2. Encourage children to pester their parents to buy things.
3. Lead children to think they will be unpopular, or not as good as others, unless they buy the product.
4. Show children behaving dangerously, for example, leaning right out of windows.

In addition, it says that when an advert shows a child and an open fire, there must be a guard in front of the fire.

What's wrong here?

Each of the three advertisements breaks at least one of the rules. For each advert:

1 Explain what it is doing wrong.
2 Say how it could be altered so that it obeys the rules.

Making up an advert

For the product described below, make up two advertisements for a comic, magazine, or TV:

1 obeying the rules
2 deliberately breaking the rules.

Product
A computerised toy robot that can be programmed to perform a number of simple tasks.

What's the problem?

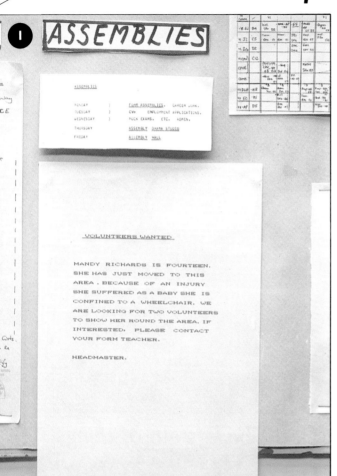

ASSEMBLIES

ASSEMBLIES

MONDAY) FORM ASSEMBLIES. CAREER JOHN.
TUESDAY) CVM EMPLOYMENT APPLICATIONS.
WEDNESDAY) MOCK EXAMS. ETC. ADMIN.
THURSDAY ASSEMBLY DRAMA STUDIO
FRIDAY ASSEMBLY HALL

VOLUNTEERS WANTED.

MANDY RICHARDS IS FOURTEEN.
SHE HAS JUST MOVED TO THIS
AREA. BECAUSE OF AN INJURY
SHE SUFFERED AS A BABY SHE IS
CONFINED TO A WHEELCHAIR. WE
ARE LOOKING FOR TWO VOLUNTEERS
TO SHOW HER ROUND THE AREA. IF
INTERESTED. PLEASE CONTACT
YOUR FORM TEACHER.

HEADMASTER.

C399 UUY

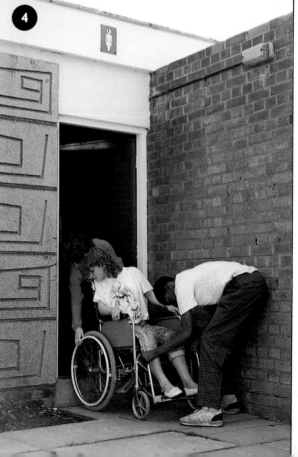

Working it out

Make a list of all the difficulties suggested in the pictures:

a) faced by the physically handicapped girl,
b) faced by the girl and boy who volunteer to help her.

What other difficulties can you think of which she might have to face in a visit to your district?

Telling the story

Think about the story that these pictures tell. Add any details you think will help to make it true to life. Give the characters names and make up the conversations they have. Now tell the whole story:

1 to a partner, as if you were one of the people in the story,

or

2 as a written story.

What about your district?

Can you think of any changes that would make it easier for a handicapped person to cope in your district?

1 Make a list of them.
2 Write a letter to your local council, mentioning the problems and listing your suggestions about what should be done. It may help to include illustrations or diagrams.

David Griffin

A The photograph shows a young man ready for the day's business at a gardening and plant stall in Hereford's Buttermarket. The young man is David Griffin and he doesn't just work at the stall, he owns it. At the age of 23 he is a car owner and driver, he runs a successful business which he has built up himself and in 1984 was a finalist in the Livewire scheme, sponsored by Shell UK, receiving an interest-free loan under the Youth Enterprise Scheme. He's been lucky, you might think, but you would be wrong. David Griffin is no ordinary young man and his story is far from straightforward.

B David was a normal, happy, healthy baby until he was one year old. At the age when most babies are learning to crawl and then walk, things started to go wrong. He seemed to be in pain, he was often sick, and had diarrhoea. The doctors were puzzled, but suggested all the obvious baby troubles: teething, tonsilitis and even gastro-enteritis. After six months of worry for his parents and numerous hospital visits and tests, it was discovered that David was suffering from rheumatoid arthritis.

C With swollen and painful joints, David couldn't walk at primary school age and used to push himself around on a little trolley. The teachers were helpful but thought that because he was physically slow, he would be mentally slow, too. At secondary school he struck lucky. One of the new comprehensive schools was being adapted to take disabled children. And David was certainly disabled, though he prefers to use the word disadvantaged. He had lost the sight in one eye at the age of three and the new wonder-drug steroid treatment had affected his growth, so that even now he is only 4′ 2″ (1.27m).

D When David was about fourteen, he wanted to increase his pocket money. He hit on the idea of selling plants. He thought this would be a good idea, because plants don't last for ever, so you can always sell more. He sold plants to the school staff and to the doctors and nurses who treated him on his frequent hospital visits. He had soon made enough money to buy a small, cheap greenhouse. It wasn't very good: it was like a plastic wigwam and it let in the wind. Soon he managed to trade it in for a proper solid greenhouse, and went on raising more and more plants.

David left school when he was seventeen, having lost a year because of all the hospital treatment he received. Although he had done well enough in his exams to look for a job, he knew exactly what he wanted to do. He rented a table in the indoor market two days a week and sold plants there. Then a proper market stall came up for sale. David had worked out that the owner was going out of business, and so he was able to buy the stall at a reasonable price. The new stall made a big difference. Instead of selling from a small table two days a week, he was able to operate from his larger stall every day except Sunday, selling plants and seeds and other goods for the garden.

F David, as well as making it clear that he has had to stand on his own feet, also gratefully acknowledges the help he has received: from teachers at his secondary school, for instance, and from a local business studies course he went on when he left school. From his experiences of illness and from learning on the job, he has found the mental toughness he needs in the business world. No local businessmen and women have cause to feel sorry for him – he can look after himself very well. He is an example of self-reliance and determination to all of us, whether or not we are disadvantaged ourselves.

Elizabeth Seely

Seeing the pattern

The story was written in 1987. It has six paragraphs, A–F. The first and the last are about David's recent life. The others are about these periods:

1965–6
1969–75
1978
1981

Which is which?

Sentence spotting

Find the sentences that tell the reader about each of these topics:

1 The disability David suffers from.
2 The effects that the disability and the treatment have had on him.
3 How David was treated at school.
4 How he started making money selling plants.
5 How his business grew.
6 What kind of person he is.

Answering questions

Answer each of these questions in your own words.

1 What does David Griffin suffer from and how has it affected him?
2 How did schools and teachers respond to David's disability?
3 How and why did he start his career selling plants?
4 What are the main stages by which his business has grown?
5 What kind of person do you think he is, and why?

Summing it all up

In what ways would you say that David provides a lesson about overcoming difficulties:

a) for disadvantaged people
b) for people who are not disadvantaged?

Taking pains

No matter how lucky you are, one difficulty you will certainly have experienced at some point in your life is coping with pain. Sometimes it is difficult to find the right words to describe an ache or a pain.

1 Can you think of reasons why this should be?

2 In what circumstances do people have to describe pains?

There are lots of different kinds of pain and there are many different words to describe them. If you have a good vocabulary, finding the right words for a particular pain is much easier.

Questions

1 Do you know what they all mean? If not, find out their meanings.
2 Can you think of any more pain words to add to the list?
3 Which word(s) would normally be used for:
   a) the pain of an insect bite
   b) the pain when you hit your thumb with a hammer
   c) the pain when a dentist's drill touches a nerve?
4 Think of three different examples of physical pain you have experienced. Say how the pain was caused and list the pain words which describe it best.

Using comparisons

Sometimes the best way of describing a pain is to compare it with something else.

IT FELT AS IF SOMEONE WAS TRYING TO SANDPAPER MY THROAT.

MY TOE FELT LIKE A HOT AIR BALLOON ABOUT TO LIFT OFF.

MY HEAD FELT AS IF SOMEONE WAS SAWING METAL IN A WIND TUNNEL.

Writing 1

Have a go at inventing comparisons to describe these pains:

1 a stomach-ache
2 an earache
3 leg cramp
4 a broken arm

Writing 2

Now try writing a poem called *The Physical Wreck* about a person with aches and pains all over. Don't worry about making it rhyme – just take pains with the descriptions!

49

Overcoming winter difficulties

Stork hero beats blizzard

Missing words

In the story that follows a number of words have been missed out. Read the story carefully and work out the most suitable word to fill each space. Write down the number of each space and against it write the word you have thought of.

An RAF rescue helicopter was twice forced down by blizzards yesterday as it —— 1 —— to take four emergency patients, including a pregnant woman, to —— 2 ——. Visibility was so bad the Sea King twice had to put down in fields to wait for a —— 3 —— in the appalling weather.

Last night 25-year-old Mrs Pat Drummond, of Grindon, near Berwick, was celebrating the —— 4 —— of a 7lb 12oz baby daughter. Both were 'doing —— 5 ——'.

The drama began when Mrs Drummond's doctors, —— 6 ——ing a difficult birth, decided she should be —— 7 —— from Berwick Infirmary to the Royal Victoria Infirmary in Newcastle upon Tyne.

An ambulance was unable to make the trip when snow
— 8 — the A1. So the helicopter was called out from RAF
Boulmer, Northumberland. First it had to — 9 — in a back
garden in the tiny village of Newton-by-the-Sea to pick up
Doctor Bill Makepeace. 'Fortunately the Sea King is a marvellous
— 10 — you can bring down anywhere,' said — 11 —
Paul Hodgson. 'The garden was no problem.'

He and his three — 12 — picked up their patients without
any mishap. It was then their — 13 — began as the weather
— 14 — on the way to Newcastle. 'Conditions were
— 15 —,' said Flight Lieutenant Hodgson last night. 'At
times we could hardly — 16 —. On two occasions we had no
alternative but to come down. We — 17 — put for 10 to 15
minutes each time and as soon as there was some relief in the
— 18 — we took off again. It took us just over an hour to
make the return — 19 — and it was hard work. But the
patients were — 20 —.'

Daily Express 14/1/87

Funny way of putting it

These short news items come from the same
newspaper. In each of them one or more
words have been altered.

1   Which words are wrong?
2   What should they be?

There was panic crying in
some shops at the news that
the biggest bakery in the west
of Scotland could only get two
of its 60 loaves out.

One of the coldest spots is the
country was the London
Weather Centre. Their
cooling system broke down.

Schoolteachers stand to lose
£10,000 if the Thames boils. A
client has a 1000 to 1 £10 bet
that he can walk across the
river between London and
Tower Bridge.

A royal recipe to beat the child
comes from Braemar near
Balmoral. . .sugarless
porridge with a bottle of
whisky.

In Kent the London-bound
carriageway of the M20 was
blocked by ice-cream. But this
did not stop a convoy of swans
crossing over to the wrong side
and   driving
oncoming ballerinas.   towards

51

Sugar Mouse

'Come on, Sarah, time to get up!' called Mrs Freeman coming into her daughter's bedroom. 'We're late this morning.'

Sarah groaned. She did not want to wake up, she had been dreaming about her pony, Sam. They had been cantering along the beach, splashing through the edges of the waves. And now...

'Sarah, it's a quarter past seven! You can't leave it any later! You've got to get up!'

'I'm not going to!'

'Come on now, don't be silly!' said her mother. She had brought up a tray and put it on the bedside table. It was not breakfast in bed – Mrs Freeman had a husband and another daughter to look after, and had no time for such luxuries. The tray contained cotton wool, spirit, a needle in a dish of sterilised water, a syringe and a bottle of insulin.

'I'm not going to have an injection!' said Sarah, and pulled the bedclothes over her head.

'You've got to,' said her mother simply.

'I haven't got to.' Her voice was muffled by the blankets. 'I haven't got to if I don't want to!'

It was bad enough having to get up to go to school, without having to stick a needle into yourself before you could do anything. What a way to start the morning!

'Injections!' she shouted, suddenly popping her head out of the clothes. 'I'm fed up with injections!'

'I'll draw it up for you,' said her mother calmly. 'Though you ought to do it yourself.'

'That's all my life is, from one injection to the next!'

Mrs Freeman ignored her and held one of the bottles upside down, just above the level of her eyes. She pushed the needle through the self-sealing top, and concentrated on drawing the exact amount into the syringe. 'There you are,' she said when she was satisfied that the quantity was right. 'Now get it over quickly.'

'I'll do it after breakfast.'

'No, the doctor said it was very important to do it first thing, before you eat.'

'I'll do it when I want,' said Sarah, raising her voice.

'Really, Sarah, I shall lose my patience. You've got to do it, and you've got to do it straight away, so you might as well accept it.'

'You're cruel to me!' Her mother had been a nurse, she was hardened to such things. It was different if you had to do it to yourself.

'There's no need to make such a fuss. I've seen five-year-olds give themselves injections.'

Sarah had heard of these five-year-olds before. 'That's different!' she muttered. They were used to it, they'd always had injections as long as they remembered. But she was not used to it, she had only started having injections when she was eleven, last summer, just before going into the first form of the secondary school. And she would never get used to it, she hated injections!

Her mother put some surgical spirit on to a piece of cotton wool. 'Where are you going to have it?' she asked, preparing to dab the spot.

Sarah pulled the bedclothes tighter around her, protecting herself from the needle. 'I don't feel well,' she said.

'Now come on, stop play-acting! You're going to school.'

Mrs Freeman took the wrist of her daughter's hand that grasped the sheet tight to her neck. 'Your pulse is quite normal.'

'I'm not going to school.'

Still holding the wrist she tried to draw the whole arm from out of the bedclothes. 'I think you ought to put it into your arm more often. You'll make the skin on your legs tough if you always put it in the same place.'

'I don't care.' In fact she wanted it to be tough, it was already getting hard and then it did not hurt so much when the needle went in.

'Well, you ought to care. You've got lovely legs, you don't want to spoil them. Perhaps you don't care now, but in a few years' time you'll be sorry if you've got blemishes on them.'

'I don't want lovely legs. I don't care.' It was stupid bothering about hard skin on your legs, she did not want to be a beauty queen.

She let her arm be drawn out, and then said, 'That's my right arm, I can't put it into that, I can only use the syringe with my right hand.'

'You ought to try using your left hand sometimes. You should use a different place each day, right leg, left leg, right arm, left arm, and then start again. Not always your right leg.'

'I can do what I like, can't I?' She remained lying on her left arm, and pulled the clothes back over her shoulder.

'Well, I've done what I can. I'll leave it all here ready for you. Be down for breakfast in five minutes or you'll have to hurry to catch the bus, and that's not good for you.'

'I might,' grunted Sarah.

When her mother had left the room, she lay in bed looking at the tray of equipment. She eyed the syringe warily, all shining metal and glass, the plunger withdrawn, the vicious point. It was repulsive, and yet fascinating in a way. On the wall behind it was the pony chart, showing the different breeds. Sam was a

Dartmoor pony, a blue roan. Her parents had given him to her last summer, as a sort of compensation for being diabetic. If she had not had this illness, she would not have had Sam. There was a slate on the other wall with an engraving of his head, his long face, and forelock hanging over his eyes. She did not like to think of him belonging to anyone else. She wanted to have Sam, and not be diabetic as well. Her eyes kept coming back to the syringe.

She heard her mother waking up Jane. She was out of bed at once, clomping heavily into the bathroom. Mrs Freeman always woke Sarah first, to give her time for her injection.

It wasn't fair! Her sister was not diabetic, as far as she knew no one on either side of the family was. Why was she? Why had she been picked on? Why was it her body that didn't make any insulin, and so had to have it injected every day?

'It's not fair!' she cried aloud.

If the first thing she had to do was have an injection, then she would delay getting up as long as possible. Perhaps that way the injection could be put off altogether.

'Are you up yet?' called her mother from outside the room. 'You can't leave it any longer.'

Reluctantly she swung her legs out of bed. She swabbed her right thigh – always the same spot – and picked up the syringe. The place was slightly swollen and glossy, with some white spots around it. She picked at the edge with the point of the needle, lifting up the skin. Then she slid it in under. The plunger seemed to stick, it was hard to push. She could only move it a little way.

Jane burst into the room.

'Get out!'

'I'm only looking for a blouse.'

Get out!'

'I'm sorry, but I . . .'

'Get out!' Sarah screamed.

Jane went, and Mrs Freeman came running up the stairs to see what was going on. They were talking on the landing.

'What did you want to go in there for?' her mother said crossly.

'I need a clean blouse.'

'You won't find one in her room.'

'Well, there wasn't one in mine.'

'You know what she's like.'

'If you can't ask your sister something. . .!'

'You know you can't.'

'I asked her politely, I said . . .'

'Just keep away from her!'

'What a family!' muttered Jane, going back to her room.

Mrs Freeman knocked on Sarah's door. 'Have you finished yet?' she called.

'I can't.'

'What do you mean, you can't?'

'It won't go in.'

Her mother entered the bedroom, and saw Sarah sitting on the edge of the bed in her nightdress, the needle sticking into her thigh and twisted under the flesh, lifting it up as the rest of the syringe hung down on to the bed.

'What's happened?'

'I think it's stuck.'

'Honestly, if you aren't careful you'll break the needle off under the skin, and then you *will* be in trouble!'

'I couldn't help it!'

'Why do you always use the same spot?'

It's *my* leg!'

'Now come on, let me see if I can get it in.' She picked up the syringe that was resting between bed and thigh, and Sarah screamed as the needle went straight. 'Don't make a fuss!'

'It's all right for you, you haven't got it sticking in your leg. You don't know what it's like, it's hurting!'

'It can't hurt much.'

But Sarah went on shouting. Her mother found that she could not move the plunger, and withdrew the needle. Once it was out, the plunger worked quite freely.

'I've never known that before,' she said. 'You'll have to have it somewhere else. Let me try it in your arm.'

'No!'

'You do it then.'

'Leave me alone!'

'You'll be late for school.'

'I'm not going to school! I'm not going to get up! I'm not going to have an injection! So leave me alone!'

John Branfield *Sugar Mouse*

Questions to think and talk about

1   What are your feelings about what Sarah has to do every morning?
2   How do you think diabetes affects her life as a whole?
3   What do you think of the way in which she is behaving on this particular morning?
4   How does her mother treat her?
5   Do you think that her mother is handling the problem in the best way?

Writing

Imagine that you have been unwell for some time. In hospital, the doctors tell you that you are diabetic and must inject yourself with insulin every day.

1   Write down your immediate thoughts and feelings.
2   Write two short conversations:
    a) with the doctor who has come to tell you,
    b) with your parents next time they come to visit you.

Charity appeal

YOUR CHANCE TO MAKE THE WORLD A BETTER PLACE...

For millions of children in developing countries, life is a constant struggle to survive. Their families are waging a continual battle against poverty. These are the kinds of problems they face:

▶ Insufficient food for their children to eat
▶ Few opportunities for education and skills training
▶ Lack of basic health care and clean water

So many people are suffering from poverty, we can often feel powerless to help. But there is something practical *you* can do to give hope to a child and community in need. Please read this leaflet to find out why you should sponsor a child.

...SPONSOR A CHILD THROUGH ACTIONAID

In this Special, you work out how to raise money for a chosen charity. To begin with, you need to choose the charity you wish to support.

Choosing a charity

There are so many good causes that it is impossible to support them all.

1   For each of the charities shown on this page, write down the reasons that might make people wish to support it.
2   Put these charities in order, so that the one you would most like to support is number 1, and so on.
3   Make a short list of charities not shown here that you think are worth supporting.
4   Using the lists that you have made, choose **one** charity that you wish to support for this exercise. Explain why you have chosen it.

A fund-raising ABC

A Auction of records, books and sports equipment

B Baby-sitting
Balloon race
Barbecue
Bed-pushing marathon
Bingo

C Carnival
Carol singing
Car-washing
Chopping firewood
Concert

D

E Empty bottle collection

F Fishing competition
Football match (Club v Celebrities)
Fortune-telling

G Go-karting

H Halloween party

I Indoor games competition

K Kiosk to sell hot dogs
Knitting (sponsored)

L Lawn-mowing

M Music festival

N Newspaper collection (for salvage)

O Outgrown clothes sale

P

Q Quiz competition

R Raffle (must be organised by an adult)
Record swaps/sales

S Sale of . . . anything you can get for nothing
Sponsored . . . anything
Sweets (made at home and then sold not eaten)

T Toy-making
Treasure hunt

U 'Universal Aunts' (people who are prepared to go anywhere and do anything, more or less, for money)

V Variety show

W Window-cleaning

X Xmas cards

Y 'Yesterdays' sale (valuable and not-so-valuable bygones collected from parents and friends and auctioned)

Z Zany ideas: race for people rolling down a hill, goldfish beauty competition.

Deciding what to do

1 There are no suggestions for D, J, or P. Think of as many fund-raising ideas as you can for each of these letters.
2 Can you think of good fund-raising ideas that are not on this list?
3 Which of all the ideas do you think would be:
   a) most fun to do?
   b) most popular with the public?
   c) likely to raise the most money?
4 Which would you most like to organise?
5 Choose the best fund-raising method for your charity. Write it down and explain why you have chosen it.

Planning the event

Now you have chosen your event, you have got to decide how to organise it. Make a list of these points:

1 Title of the event.
2 Brief details of what it involves.
3 Jobs that have to be done before it can take place.
4 Equipment needed and where you are going to get it from.
5 Any special permission or help needed.
6 Any money needed for these preparations, and some idea of where you will get it from.

Publicity

You will also need to publicise your event, so that as many people as possible know about it and want to take part.

1 Can you think of ways of publicising your event?
2 For each of the methods in the illustration, and any others that you have thought of, answer these questions:

a) How much does it cost?
b) How much work is required?
c) How many people are needed for it?
d) Are there any problems connected with it?
e) How big an audience will it reach?
f) Are the cost and effort worth it?

3 Decide how you will publicise your event and explain how you will go about it.
4 Make up one of the following for your event:
   newspaper advertisement
   publicity leaflet
   short radio advertisement.

Running the event

Think about how your event will be organised. Make a list of the following:

1. Different jobs to be done.
2. People required to do the jobs.
3. Equipment required.
4. Where you are going to get the equipment from.
5. How you will deal with the money that you take in.
6. Anything else that needs to be done.

Writing a report

Your event has taken place and it has been a great success. Write **one** of the following, describing what happened:

> a letter to a friend
> a newspaper report
> a report for local radio.

59

Changing places

Each of these photographs illustrates an aspect of changing places. For each one answer these questions.

1 What is happening?
2 Why does it illustrate 'changing places'?
3 What do you think are the main thoughts and feelings of the person in the picture?

Most of us have changed places in one way or another at some time in our lives. How about you?

Make a chart of the main changes that have happened to you.

	When I was	Changes	Memories
①	5 years old	School !!!	Frightened and upset, but in a few days I fitted in.
②	7 years old	I appeared in my first pantomime.	The excitement and fun of the stage atmosphere.
③	10 years old	Asked to film (as an extra) in Robin of Sherwood.	An enthralling new experience. I have many memories of this.
④	11 years old	Took part in a	I won a gold and

Writing autobiography

Autobiography is writing the story of your own life. If you've ever tried writing your autobiography, you may have found it hard to decide what to include and what to leave out. One idea is to organise your writing around the times when you have changed places in some way.

Use the chart you have made to help you write a piece of autobiography.

A piece of my autobiography

When I was ten years old I did a lot of dancing and acting. You name it, I did it! Anyway, one day my dancing teacher asked me if I would like to appear, as an extra, in the series Robin of Sherwood. Of course I was delighted and accepted the offer.

I remember the long coach journey to a huge park where the filming would take place. I was feeling sick, my stomach turning upside-down. When we arrived we were taken to a portable cabin where we changed into the old clothes we were given. Our faces were plastered with charcoal and our hair matted with mousse! I remember a lot of waiting around. The producer often got a bit fraught (to say the least) with the main characters.

Comfort goes to Ghana

Comfort is the twelve-year-old daughter of Mante, a black Ghanaian, and Margaret, a white English woman. She has lived most of her life in London, but then her mother was killed in a road accident. Since then she has lived with her English grandparents in a village in Sussex, and with her father in Accra, the capital city of Ghana. Now she is arriving with her Aunt Ata in Wanwangeri, the village where she is to meet her Ghanaian grandmother for the first time. Comfort is not sure what to expect.

Comfort had never been as tired as the evening she followed Ata down the sandy track that led to Wanwangeri the following day. The village was not so very far from Accra but for every hour they had spent actually travelling they had spent two or three in lorry parks, drinking orange and eating roasted plantain*, waiting in the shade of trees for the next lorry to fill up. Ata showed no impatience. She was used to it and enjoyed greeting friends and exchanging gossip. When it grew hot she spread her cloth and lay down with her bundle under her head and went to sleep.

'Are we nearly there?' Comfort said. They had had to walk from Akwapawa and her neck ached from the case and her feet were sore.

'Soon-soon we come to your grandmother's compound*,' Ata said walking ahead down the narrow track. Between the trees Comfort could see huts and fences made of palm fronds, dried brown and brittle in the sun. Skinny cats and small white chickens scattered in front of them and children stared.

Ata turned towards a fence which was higher than its neighbouring fences and pushed her way through and Comfort followed. Inside it was like another smaller village, a dozen huts made of red swish*, each one belonging to a different member of the family. One hut was used as a kitchen and the children were all gathered round, watching hungrily as the evening meal, the main meal of the day, was cooked by Esi on a kerosene stove. As soon as they saw Ata, they ran round her, clapping and jumping, her own children and the children of Esi, her sister. For a moment Comfort seemed forgotten but as the hubbub subsided Ata said, 'I have brought Comfort, child of Mante.'

'Welcome, Comfort,' the ten children gazed at her round-eyed and the smaller ones pressed forward to touch her hands. The older ones went to school in neat uniforms, but at home they

*plantain banana-like fruit of a tropical tree.
*compound fenced-off area of the village. There is one compound for women and girls and one for men and boys.
*swish cane used for the walls and roofs of huts.

wore ancient shorts or cloths wound round their waists. Several
had livid pink patches on their legs where cuts had festered but
they all smiled widely.

'Ama, take care of Comfort,' Ata said. She stood holding her
youngest child, a five year old called Bolo on her hip.

'Come,' Ama said detaching herself from the younger children
and leading Comfort into one of the huts. Inside, the thatched
roof was high and sloped steeply which made it surprisingly cool.
There were sleeping mats rolled and stacked against the wall, a
hook from which hung a mirror, several low carved stools but no
other furniture except a box against the wall in which Ama kept
her clothes. Comfort put her striped case beside it, carefully.

'Where is my grandmother?' she asked in Ga.

'She stays in her hut and sleeps when it is hot,' Ama said. A
small girl came to the door carrying a cup of drinking water from
the round calabash* between her two hands and stood watching
as Comfort drank it. The water was cool and tasted slightly of
wood ash. 'Is she my cousin too?' Comfort said as the child
scampered away.

*calabash dried shell of a large
 fruit, used as a container
 for water.

63

'Tawia?' Ama seemed surprised and held up her fingers to explain. 'She is your sister like I am your sister. Our mother and your father are brother and sister so of course we are sisters too, that way there is peace and happiness in the family.'

'Oh, I see,' said Comfort pleased to find Ama was her *sister*, that according to this reckoning she had lots of brothers and sisters. Ama squatted on her heels beside Comfort's case. She was a year older than Comfort and a shade taller, her breasts small bumps under her cloth. Her hair was short and her eyes wide, she had small gold ear-rings like Comfort's own. 'Is your father's hut here too?'

'Of course not,' Ama snorted with merriment. 'He lives in the men's compound. How can a man talk wisely if he lives with children who chatter like monkeys? It is good you come here, very good. We talk every night before we go to sleep, yes?' Ama's smile was open and completely friendly. 'You tell me about England, yes, and I tell you about Wanwangeri and which boys are nice, yes? For a long time my sister, Yaa, Esi's daughter, slept in this hut with me but now she is married and gone to her husband's village. Aye-aye, I was sad that day but now you come and I am glad. We will go to the market together each day?'

'Don't you go to school?' Comfort asked.

'School?' Ama laughed. 'I am thirteen years old, how can I go

to school with so many children here, water to fetch, food to cook?' She talked in the same dramatic way as her mother, gesturing with her hands. 'Besides I must go to the market with my mother or Esi and there is much to learn before I am fit to be a woman.'

'Which is Grandmother's hut?' Comfort asked twisting the amulet that hung round her neck. Ama pointed to a hut made of red swish like the others but with a pattern of wide black and white bands painted on the outside walls and a curtain of plastic ribbons across the doorway instead of a sack. Outside Esi called that the food was ready and began scooping it from the big cooking pots into bowls.

'Come, you will see Grandmother now and I must take food to my father,' Ama said. Wives took it in turns to cook for their husbands and daughters carried the food across. Ama took the first bowl and disappeared out of the gate and the younger girl, Tawia, took the next bowl and followed Ama out. Everyone was served in a particular order according to their age, Bolo was one of the smallest and he and the other children waited patiently though their eyes watched the food. Esi handed two bowls to Comfort.

'Give this to Grandmother,' she said.

'Suppose she is still asleep?' Comfort murmured shyly but

Grandmother was already coming out of her hut. She looked older than Comfort had imagined and she was taller too. Her face was thin, hawk-like as she stood leaning on her stick and staring at Comfort with bright black eyes.

'Aye-aye, my been-to granddaughter has come at last,' she muttered in Ga, she spoke no English, and sighed with a deep satisfaction as if something was at last completed. 'An only palm fruit does not get lost in the fire.'

'Greetings to you, Grandmother. I have been wanting to see you for a long time. Thank you for the amulet*, it has brought me good luck already if it has brought me here to see you,' Comfort said, aware that this was an important moment. She spoke in the way Mante had taught her. The words were waiting ready on her tongue.

'Aye-aye, the child speaks well. She is truly Mante's child. Were there not always plenty of sweet words in Mante's mouth?' her grandmother enquired of the compound.

'My father sends his greetings. He hopes to visit you soon,' Comfort added.

'Pshaw, greetings cost nothing,' Grandmother said settling herself on one of the stools in front of her hut and waving Comfort to sit on another. 'Now eat, child.'

Comfort was hungry. There had been plenty of snacks and drinks during the journey to Wanwangeri but it was the first solid meal she had had in two days. She had never eaten *kenke**
before but now she broke a bit from the soft white lump with her fingers and scooped it into the meat and vegetable stew under her grandmother's critical gaze.

'Aye-aye, Mante's child eats with her fingers, eh?' she said with a derisive chuckle and she began to eat herself, rolling her *kenke* delicately into a ball the size of a chestnut before she dipped it in the stew. Was that the correct way, Comfort wondered, watching carefully and doing the same. It was quiet in the compound then. Talking at meal times was bad manners and such bad manners could make your father die. The ten children ate in silence, washing their bowls when they had finished and slipping out of the compound.

Grandmother finished eating and closed her eyes. She seemed to be asleep with her back propped against the wall of the hut. Could she slip away now, Comfort wondered. She wanted to talk to Ama and see the rest of Wanwangeri but every time she stirred her grandmother stirred too. The sun sank behind the palm trees and shadows lengthened and the boys carried their father's stools to the shade tree in the centre of the village where everybody met and talked. Only Esi and Ata sat gossiping quietly in the corner near the kitchen, each with a small child asleep on her lap.

*amulet charm to keep off evil spirits or to bring good luck. It is usually a small trinket attached to a bracelet or necklace.

*kenke kind of dumpling made from fermented maize flour. It is eaten with stew.

Comfort stood up and Grandmother opened her eyes at once, 'I worked for Mante day and night, paying for his schooling, my youngest son,' Grandmother said. 'Is it the will of Onyame that a child send his mother a blue letter from England to break her heart?'

'What blue letter?' Comfort whispered.

'What blue letter?' Grandmother repeated rocking backwards and forwards as she remembered her sadness. 'The blue letter which tells that he has married a white woman in that London place. A father and mother must choose a bride first time, what can a young man know of such things? How can we find out if the girl is healthy and respectable and can cook as a wife should cook? A child was born in London and lost to us,' Grandmother hugged her arms tight across her chest and her eyes circled the quiet compound, rested a moment on Ata and Esi and the sleeping children and came back to Comfort. Beyond the palm-frond fence there was drumming now, a soft throbbing that was part of the Wanwangeri darkness.

'But now that child has come,' Grandmother said softly. 'How can a son stand against Onyame and his own mother? At last you have come to me, Comfort.'

Geraldine Kaye *Comfort Herself*

Thinking about the story

1   Think about what Comfort's life may have been like in London. Make a list of the differences between that London life and the life of her cousins in Wanwangeri.
2   What will Comfort know that her cousins do not know?
3   What will they know that she doesn't know?
4   Why do you think Comfort's grandmother is so pleased that Comfort has come to Wanwangeri?
5   What are your first impressions of the grandmother?
6   Do you think Comfort copes well with the first meeting?
7   Read the last paragraph again. Can you guess who or what Onyame is?

Drawing and writing

1   Look carefully at the information in the passage about the village. Draw a map of the village and label the different sections.
2   Comfort keeps a diary. Write her diary entry for her first day in Wanwangeri. Include her impressions of:
     the village
     the different customs
     her cousins
     her grandmother.

Other people's shoes

One of the interesting things about telling and writing stories is that you can change places with a person you have invented. In stories you can put yourself in the place of any kind of person you like, and you can have adventures you'd never have in real life.

When you are making up a story there are two main ways of changing places with a character.

Telling it as 'I'

Penelope Lively is a well-known author. She writes stories for adults and children.

In Princess by Mistake, *Penelope Lively imagines that she is a man. He is remembering his past...*

...when he was a small boy:

A long time ago, when I was young, on a Wednesday afternoon, a very strange thing happened to me. So strange, you probably won't believe it. That's up to you. Anyway, this is what happened. I know it was a Wednesday, because we always went to the library on Wednesday afternoons, my mother, my sister Sally and I. And all the way home from the library my sister Sally and I had a fight...

Penelope Lively   *Princess by Mistake*

A story told in this way is called a **first person story**.

Writing from a point of view

The second way of putting yourself in the place of one of your characters is to tell the story **about** him or her, but to do it from his or her **point of view**.

Waiting for the boat made Steven lonely. He could hear the silence behind him in the trees of Freeman's Wood. He listened to the silence until he could hear it humming darkly amongst the wet black branches, and he began to be afraid. What if *Rosa* was lost at sea? What if Jakey could not find his way back through the mist? The darkness was coming on. Soon it would be all about him, and he would be alone in this silent place of marsh and river and winter trees.

Janni Howker *Jakey* from *Badger on the Barge*

Janni Howker isn't pretending to be Steven as she tells the story, but she **is** telling us about all his thoughts and feelings. We see, hear and feel what he does.

Questions

1 What are the advantages of a first person story
   a) for the reader?
   b) for the writer?
2 What are the disadvantages?
3 Look back at the extract from *Comfort Herself*.
   a) Is Comfort telling the story herself?
   b) Find any sentences you can which show us what Comfort is secretly thinking, or which show us things from her point of view? Write down three examples.

Writing

1 Try continuing the story by Penelope Lively. You will have to pretend to be the 'I' (a boy) telling the story.
2 Continue the story by Janni Howker. Write **about** the boy, describing his thoughts and feelings.
3 Make up a story of your own called *Changing Places*. Make the main character someone who is completely different from yourself. Decide whether it will be a first person story, or one in which you write from the character's point of view, but describe them as 'he' or 'she'.

The playground

Mr Underhill has a young son. His wife has recently died and his sister has suggested that it is about time that the son should be taken to the public playground. On his way home from work, Mr Underhill stops to look at the playground.

Now he saw the children! They were dashing across the Playground meadow, fighting, pummelling, scratching, falling, every wound bleeding or about to bleed or freshly caked over. A dozen cats thrown among sleeping dogs could not have shrieked as loud. With incredible clarity, Mr Underhill saw the tiniest cuts and scabs on knees and faces.

He weathered the first blast of sound, blinking. His nostrils took over when his eyes and ears retired in panic.

He sniffed the cutting odours of salve, raw adhesive, camphor, and pink Mercurochrome, so strong it lay bitter on his tongue. An iodine wind blew through the steel fence wires which glinted dully in the grey light of the overcast day. The rushing children were hell cut loose in a vast pinball table, colliding, and banging, a totalling of hits and misses, thrusts and plungings to a grand and as yet unforeseen total of brutalities.

A pen of misery, thought Underhill. Why do children insist on making life horrible for each other? Oh, the continual torture. He heard himself sigh with immense relief. Thank God, childhood was over and done for him. No more pinchings, bruisings, senseless passions and shattered dreams.

Underhill stood bemused by what he saw. If you watched for half an hour there wasn't a face in the entire enclosure that didn't wince, cry, redden with anger, pale with fear, one moment or another. Really! who said Childhood was the best time of life when in reality it was the most terrible, the most merciless era, the barbaric time when there were no police to protect you, only parents preoccupied with themselves and their taller world.

So this was the Playground where my son will play, thought Mr Underhill. So this is it.

Ray Bradbury *The Playground*

Back in the playground blues

Dreamed I was in a school playground, I was about four feet high
Yes dreamed I was back in the playground, and standing about four feet high
The playground was three miles long and the playground was five miles wide

It was broken black tarmac with a high fence all around
Broken black dusty tarmac with a high fence running all around
And it had a special name to it, they called it The Killing
Ground.

Got a mother and a father, they're a thousand miles away
The Rulers of The Killing Ground are coming out to play
Everyone thinking: who are they going to play with today?

> You get it for being Jewish
> Get it for being black
> Get it for being chicken
> Get it for fighting back
> You get it for being big and fat
> Get it for being small
> O those who get it get it and get it
> For any damn thing at all

Sometimes they take a beetle, tear off its six legs one by one
Beetle on its black back rocking in the lunchtime sun
But a beetle can't beg for mercy, a beetle's not half the fun

Heard a deep voice talking, it had that iceberg sound;
'It prepares them for Life' – but I have never found
Any place in my life that's worse than The Killing Ground.

Adrian Mitchell

Questions

Both these pieces are written from the point of view of adults looking back at childhood.

1   Do they take the same view of the playground?
2   What are the main things they agree about?
3   Are there any important differences between their views? If so, what are they?
4   Do they give an accurate view, or are they exaggerating?
5   Does the playground 'prepare them for life'? If so, how?

Writing

In Ray Bradbury's story, Mr Underhill is offered the chance of changing places with his son and going into the Playground instead of him. What do you think happens? Study both pieces of writing carefully and then tell the story.

Giving your reasons

The subject of an argument often boils down to a question, such as:

Is it better to be 15 or 25?

Do you agree that nowadays schools do not teach children what they really need to know?

Is it better to live in the country or a city?

If you express the subject of an argument as a question, it is easier to see that:

1 There are always at least two possible points of view.
2 It isn't good enough just to answer 'Yes' or 'No'. You must give **reasons**. Unless you do this, you'll never be able to persuade other people to agree with you.

Is it better to be 15 or 25?

1 Copy out diagram A. (Allow plenty of space.) Then add as many points as you can think of in each of the four spaces, as in B.
2 Now take each of your points as a heading. Underneath each heading add more points connected to it, which either support it or go against it.
3 Read through all the notes you have. Decide on the best order for the points you want to make. Number them in this order.
4 Now you are ready to begin to present your argument. This could be in speech, for example, in a class discussion or debate. Or it could be in writing. If so, you may want to write more than one draft. See page 117 about this.

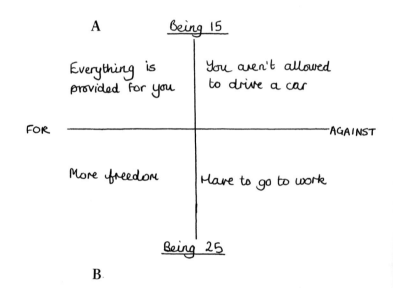

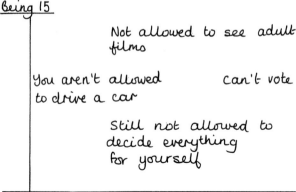

Equality of the sexes

All things being equal

At last women can claim the right to have a family or a career: or a family *and* a career. Women are becoming leaders in industry, politics and social welfare. It seems no door is closed to the modern woman.

Figures released today show that

Read carefully what is said in the magazine article and in the two letters.

1 Make a list of the points made by Ms Perowski in her letter.
2 Make a list of the points made by Mr Young in his letter.
3 **Think:** Can men and women ever be equal? Are they equal now? Write down your own views on this subject. You can mention any of the points made in the letters, if you wish, but use as many of your own ideas as possible.

Dear Sir/Madam

I object most strongly to your article, 'All Things Being Equal'.

The male attitude which has existed for centuries has not really changed at all. Women are not given jobs which they deserve, and for which they are highly qualified, simply because they *are* women.

A man may say he regards male and female equally, but just wait until he is looking for someone for an important job. Then you will find out what his feelings really are!

The idea that 'a woman's place is in the home' still rules. The article which you printed gives a false impression entirely and has caused great distress to me and many of my friends.

The writer of the article, obviously a man, seems to think that women's battle for equality is over. I promise you, the battle has just begun.

Sandra Perowski (Ms)

Dear Sir/Madam

I object most strongly to your article, 'All Things Being Equal'.

The writer of this article, obviously a woman, seems very pleased with herself. It is not surprising that she is, since the examples given in the article have been chosen very carefully.

There is no mention of the stupid side of this so-called equality: women's football, women's tug-of-war, women's weight-lifting, and so on. I suppose the next thing we shall have to have is men's netball and men's sewing circles. It is ridiculous. The whole thing has gone too far.

Women only want the attractive jobs where they don't break their fingernails. When did you last see a women coalminer, or a women digging a hole in the road? Oh, no, they won't do that. Leave the dirty jobs for us men, that's their motto.

Fred Young

Typewriting class

Dear Miss Hinson

I am spitting

In front of my typewriter

With the rest of my commercesnail sturdy students

Triping you tHis later.

The truce is MissHinson

I am not happy with my cross.

Every day on Woundsday

I sit in my dusk

With my typw rutter

Trooping without lurking at the lattice

All sorts of weird messengers.

To give one exam Pill,

'The quick down socks ...

The quick brine pox ...

The sick down jocks

Humps over the hazy bog'

When everyone Knows

That a sick down jock

Would nottbe seen dead

Near a hazy bog.

Another one we tripe is

'Now is the tame

For all guide men

TO Cram to the head

Of the pratty.'

To may Way of thinking

If that is all you Get to tripe

IN true whelks of sturdy

Then I am thinking of changing

To crookery classes.

I would sooner end up a crook

Than a shirt hand trappist

Amy day die of the wink.

I have taken the tremble, Miss Hinson

To trip you this later

So tat you will be able

TO understand my indi gnation.

I must clothe Now

As the Bill is groaning

Yours fitfully....

Gareth Owen

What did he mean to type?

Changing clothes

Carol, Trish, Anna and Suzy like changing clothes. One day Carol swapped shoes with Suzy and Anna exchanged jeans with Trish. Carol wore Anna's blouse and Anna passed Carol's blouse to Trish, and then put on Trish's blouse herself. Trish and Suzy swapped hats and so did Anna and Carol.

Before all this started, each of them was wearing hat, blouse, jeans and shoes of one colour. Carol was in white, Trish in red, Anna wore green and Suzy was all in blue.

Can you describe what each of them is wearing now?

Changing words

Can you change Love to Hate? It's easy if you do it letter by letter:

> LOVE
> HOVE
> HAVE
> HATE

Now do the same with these. Try to find the shortest route using the fewest number of changes.

> HILL → LAKE
> TENT → CAVE
> LIVE → DEAD
> HAND → FOOT

Remember you can only change one letter at a time and you must always make a proper word.

Anagrams

Each of these groups of words is an anagram of an author's name. All the authors have written poems or stories in this book.

> NOW THE RAGE
> UPEND HAL
> A LARGE KIND EYE
> ELLA'S WET BIKE
> PEEL OPEN VILELY

Journey to Asfodelia

SPECIAL D

Time Travel International
2648 East 94th Street
New York
USA

23rd March 1995

THURSDAY 20th Au...
I have decided to take
with me a small
"emergency kit"... I
is against orders – a
may even damage the
working of the time
machine, but I'm going
to risk it...
If I get into any kind
of trouble, those few
things may help me
survive ...

You have been selected as one of the first non-
American citizens to take part in Time Travel
Experiments. As you know, the system of time travel has
now been perfected by American scientists and it has
been decided to invite selected non-Americans to take
part in these experiments.
Please let us know as soon as possible if you
wish to take up this invitation. We will then send you
further information about training and the personnel to
accompany you on your trip.

Yours faithfully,

William J. Hersey Jnr, Mission Director

Time Travel International
2648 East 94th Street
New York
USA

15th May 1995

Details of Mission 142A have now been finalised:

Target Date: 2167
Target Area: The planet Asfodelia
Start of mission: 23rd August 1995
Personnel dossiers of mission members encl...
Start details:

NAME

AGE

EXPERIENCE

NAME

What to do

You are a member of the experiment team. You will be travelling through time with two companions. As you go through the project, you will make up a series of documents that tell the story of what happens.

1   Think about the three people who will be selected to go with you on this journey: what are they like? Make up personnel dossiers for:
a) yourself
b) each of your three companions.

2   Think about how you and your family feel on the day that you hear that you have been selected. You decide to keep a diary of what happens. Write the entry for 17 May 1995.
3   Make up a list of the things you would take in your personal survival kit. The container they will be kept in is only 20cm × 15cm × 3cm.
4   No details are given of how the time travel works. Decide for yourself what happens to you on 23 August 1995. Then write your diary for that day.

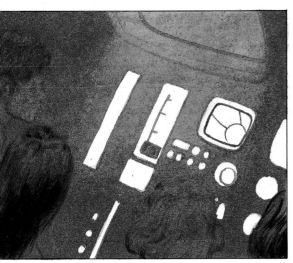

Exploring Asfodelia

You arrive on the planet Asfodelia.

Writing

Describe what you can see in each direction and your thoughts and feelings about this new planet.

Looking south-west

Making decisions

You must decide what to do:

1 Will you stay together or divide up? What are the advantages and disadvantages?
2 In which direction(s) will you go?
3 Why?

Writing

When you have made up your mind, record what has happened in your personal diary. Then describe how you started to explore Asfodelia.

Looking north

Looking south-east

Encounters

This page tells the story of what happens next as you explore Asfodelia. What happens to you depends on the choice you made at the beginning of the journey. There are three stories. Each one starts at the top of the page and goes down. You have to follow the direction which you chose on page 78–9.

What to do

1   Work out which column you have to follow.
2   Study the pictures and work out what happens to your party.

Writing

Write your diary, telling the story of what happens in pictures 1–3.

What do we do now?

1   Study pictures 4 and 5. You are facing a group of completely unknown creatures. You need to think...quickly!
2   How would you find out whether these creatures are friendly or hostile?
3   How would you try to communicate with them?
4   How would you try to make sure that you are not injured or captured?
5   Think about the answers to these questions and make a plan of action.

Writing

Now tell the story in your diary of what happened when you met the creatures, and carried out your plan.

Travelling north

Travelling south-west

Travelling south-east

Confusions

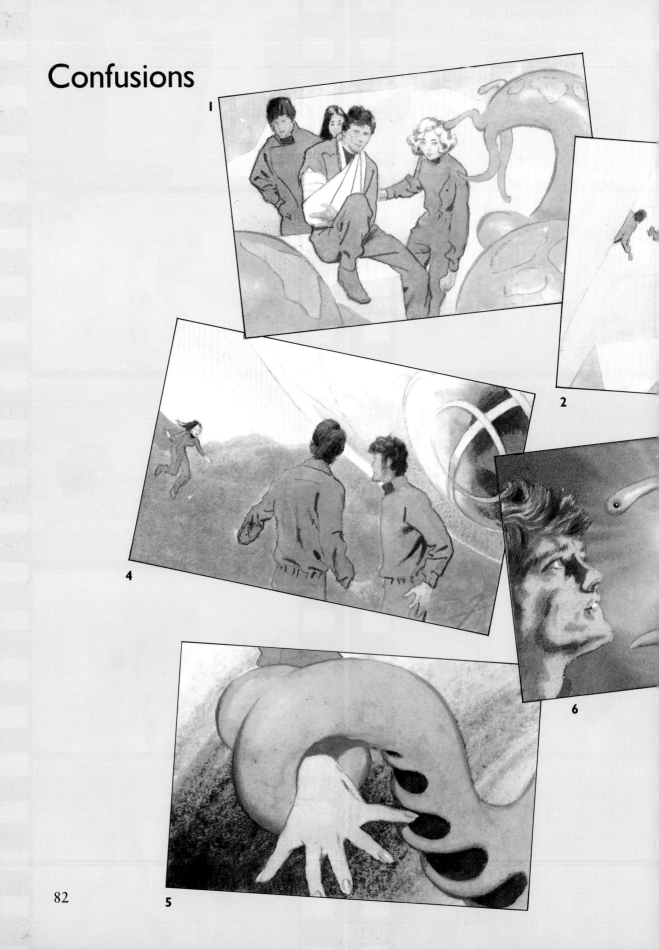

1

2

4

5

6

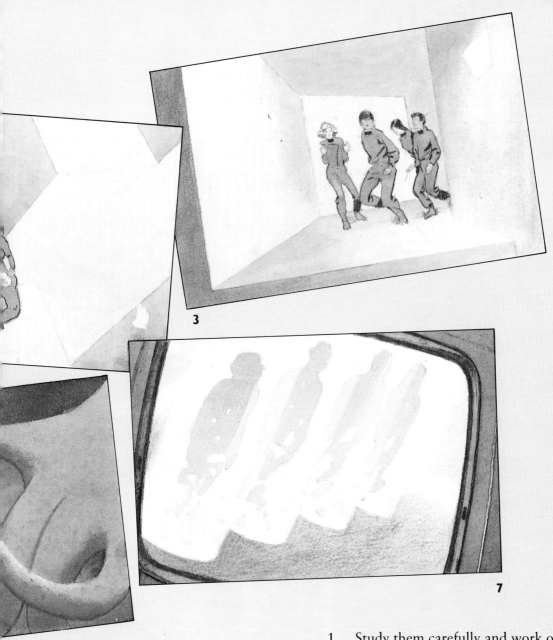

3

7

Puzzling it out

These pictures tell how the story ends.
Picture number 1 shows the next part of it,
and Picture number 7 shows the end.
Unfortunately Pictures 2, 3, 4, 5, 6 are not in
the right order.

1   Study them carefully and work out what
    you think has happened.
2   Write down the numbers of the pictures
    in that order.

Writing

Now write your personal diary, telling the
story of what happened and how you got
back to Earth in 1995.

Life-style

	Styles	Words	Things	Pastimes
1950s	polo-neck sweaters *Brylcream*	cool hip supersonic dig-it	hula-hoops yo-yos horror comics roller-skates	
1960s	mods hippies kipper ties chelsea boots chisel-toes	fab groovy square 'man' with-it wow swinging	tower blocks ring roads colour supplements universities	
1970s	Habitat stripped pine pop punk vests Afro hair skinhead	right-on way-out triffic pigs super too much	breathalysers double glazing trannies QE2 training shoes Concorde	
1980s	short hair high tech Sloane Ranger gay New Romantic	laid back no-way naff brill wally	personal computers Walkman radios	

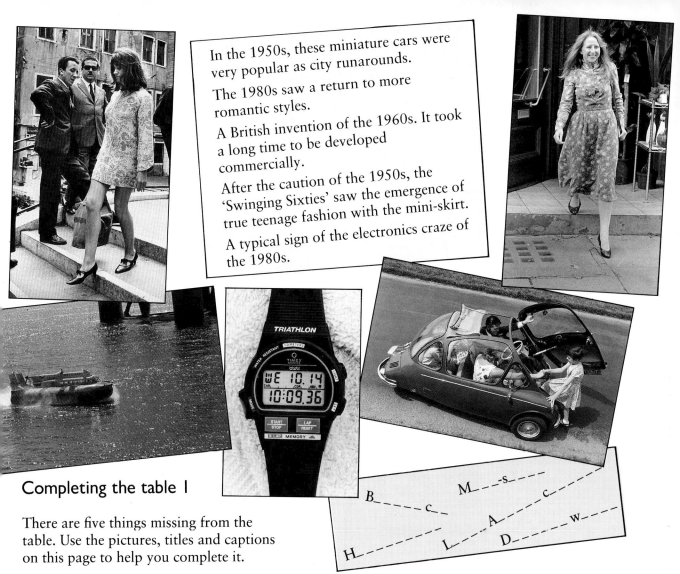

In the 1950s, these miniature cars were very popular as city runarounds.

The 1980s saw a return to more romantic styles.

A British invention of the 1960s. It took a long time to be developed commercially.

After the caution of the 1950s, the 'Swinging Sixties' saw the emergence of true teenage fashion with the mini-skirt.

A typical sign of the electronics craze of the 1980s.

Completing the table 1

There are five things missing from the table. Use the pictures, titles and captions on this page to help you complete it.

Completing the table 2

1   In the Pastimes column on the opposite page there should be two items for each decade, taken from this list:

jogging	real ale
bingo	ten-pin bowling
fast food	pop festivals
coffee bars	jiving

Which items do you think should be in which space?

2   These three clothing styles have been left out. Where should they go?

hot pants   hipsters   duffel coats

3   These three things have been left out. Where should they go?

skateboards   scooters   BMX bikes

Up-to-date

The table only covers the early years of the 1980s. What should be added to cover the period up to the present day? Make a list of items to go into each column. Write a sentence or two about each one.

Future trends

As you can see, today's fashion can look very strange in a few years' time. Tomorrow's fashion would look even stranger today... if we knew what it was going to be. Make up a style table to cover one of these decades:

1990s   2010s
2000s   2020s

Styles of language

Language changes as the years go by. New words are born and old ones die. Some words last a long time, while others, like fashions, are soon worn out.

The lady's castle

In the fourteenth century people in Britain spoke a language that seems strange to us now. Even so, we can see that it is something like modern English.

What does it mean?

Hire to disport means 'to enjoy herself'.

1. How many of the other words can you recognise?
2. What do you think each of the captions means?
3. Study the pictures and the captions. Work out the meaning of these words and phrases: hire   heigh
   faste   seigh
   seillinge hir cours
4. Write modern English captions to go with the pictures.

Now stood hire castel faste by the see

And often with hire freendes walketh shee

Hire to disporte, upon the bank an heigh

Where as she many a ship and barge seigh seillinge hir cours

Rhyming slang

Most people know how rhyming slang works. Instead of using the usual word for something, you use a phrase that rhymes with it. Often you only use the first word of the phrase, so that the slang becomes a kind of code:

Feet = plates of meat = plates
As in 'I must take the weight off me plates.'

Each of these sentences contains one piece of rhyming slang. Some of them are very old. To help you, they haven't been shortened.

What does each sentence mean.

1. 'It's expensive mind – it'll cost you a Lady Godiva.'
2. 'He was sprawled out in his lion's lair, dead to the world.'
3. 'She was dressed up to the nines – she had a lean and fat that would've done at Ascot.'
4. 'That boy would forget anything. Yesterday he went to school without wearing his lamb's fry.'
5. 'It must be true: I read it in the linen draper.'

86

The Swinging Sixties

Each age produces its own special words to describe the things it likes and dislikes. This is how people might have spoken in the 1960s.

A: Hey man – that's just cool.
B: You dig?
A: Groovy, man, groovy.

A: Hey, that's trendy innit?
B: Looks a bit kinky to me.
A: I think it's fab. I wish I had one.
B: You'd look really grotty in it.

Fashionable?

The conversations include these words:

cool   trendy   fab   groovy
dig   kinky   grotty

1   Are any of these words still used?
2   Which words would you use to replace the words that are out of date?

A guide to modern English

In a few years' time, or even next year, many of the words you use to describe clothes, music and other people will be out of fashion. Think about the words that are fashionable now. Then copy and complete this table of fashionable words.

	words to show you approve	words to show you disapprove
People		
Clothes		
Music		
Other things		

Suitable language

A: Good morning.
B: Hello.
C: Hi!
D: How do you do.

Which is which?

The four pictures show the same girl greeting different people.

1   Which greeting goes with which picture?
2   Why do you think this?

3   Why do we have different ways of greeting different people? Why don't we speak in the same way to everyone we meet?

Asking for help

A: Excuse me.
B: Yes, young lady, what can I do for you?
A: Could you help me? I don't understand this.
B: What's that?
A: It's this timetable. It doesn't seem to make sense.

A: Please Miss James.
B: Yes, what is it?
A: I can't do this one.
B: Which one?
A: This one, Miss. Could you explain it again, please?

A: 'Ere Dave.
B: Yeah – wodja want?
A: You done this one?
B: Which one?
A: This one. You got the answer?

Questions

1 What are the main ways in which these three conversations differ?
2 Why are there these differences?
3 What would happen if the girl spoke to the teacher in the way that she speaks in the third conversation? Why would this happen?

Writing

'I treat everyone the same. I don't care who it is: I don't believe in behaving and speaking differently for different people. What's more, I always tell the truth.' Make up a short story about someone who behaves like this with sad, or funny, or disastrous results.

89

Rom with grai

Rom with jukals

A traveller's life

Travelling people live a life that is very different from that of gaujos. Unlike gaujos, they don't like being cooped up in a small house and staying in the same place all the time. Instead they prefer to travel the country, earning a living as they go. In the past most travellers used horse-drawn wagons, but nowadays most have trailers pulled by transits or lorries. Although these trailers have gas cookers, just like any gaujo caravan, many travelling juvals and roms often prefer to live, eat and cook out of doors. They use a traditional open fire with props or tripods to take their kettles and cooking-pots.

Although the travellers now usually use motor vehicles to get them around the country, they are still fond of animals. If you visit an atchin'-tan, you will often see one or two grais tied up near the lorries, and maybe a rom setting off with his jukal in search of rabbits for the pot. It's true that travellers still eat hotchiwichis, but they do not bake them in clay as gaujos believe. Instead, they shave off the spines, clean them, soak them and then roast them over a fire.

They earn a living in a number of ways. Traditionally the roms have been dealers, buying and selling horses, vehicles and scrap metal. The juvals and raklies used to go from door to door, selling pegs and posies of flowers and some still do. At fair time, they can make a lot of money duckerin', as people still like to have their palms read and know what is in store for them.

The life of the travellers can be hard, and it certainly isn't one that would appeal to a lot of gaujos. But they say, 'Once a traveller, always a traveller' and it's true that despite the hostility of the authorities, the travellers continue to follow their own independent style of life.

roadside atchin'-tan

Romany juval with chavvies

traditional waggon

Words and meanings

Look at the pictures and read the text.
Copy and complete this table.

Romany word	English word
atchin'-tan	
chavvie	
duckerin'	
gaujo	
grai	
hotchiwichi	
jukal	
juval	
raklie	young woman, girl
rom	

Studying the text

Among other things, the text contains
information about:

a) Changes in the travellers' way of life.
b) How the travellers like to keep links with
   the old ways of doing things.
c) The ideas and attitudes of non-travellers.

For each of these three topics:

1 Find the sentences that are about the
   topic.
2 Explain briefly in your own words what
   is said about it.

Your opinion

People often complain about travellers,
saying that they make a mess and that they
should stop travelling and live a 'normal'
life. What is your opinion, and what are
your reasons for it?

Fashion show

Breinton High School is having its annual fashion show in aid of the School Fund. Unfortunately there's a problem with the public address system: the recorded commentary that describes all the clothes has been damaged. Can you sort it out?

Anita is wearing a cotton space-suit in fluorescent lime-green. It has full . . . . . . with tight cuffs and waist. The trousers are full but tight below the knee. Anita is wearing long soft leather . . . . . . in a shade of silver grey. When she goes dancing, Anita adds a grass skirt threaded with . . . . . . that catch the light and make music as she moves.

Jake has on . . . . . . blue denim trousers, elasticated for ease of movement. His jacket is in an Elizabethan style, made of navy polyester with tight sleeves and a tight . . . . . . It flares suddenly over the hips and as he walks we catch glimpses of the red satin . . . . . . Just the style for discos.

And now the . . . . . . look. Candy's dress is ideal for colourful leisure wear. She's wearing a . . . . . . robe in deep violet red. Over this she has on three overlapping tabards in a range of . . . . . . from the palest shade of pink through to mid-crimson.

Japheth and Mary are . . . . . . the new school uniform which has been designed by the Chairperson of the school governors. The basic uniform, which is . . . . . . consists of a polo-neck . . . . . . in blue, with matching denim jeans and canvas velcro-fastening ankle boots. Over this pupils wear a . . . . . . button-through drill lab-coat. The colour can be chosen from: red, green, yellow, and orange. As you can see, Japheth is wearing the uniform without the . . . . . ., while Mary is wearing a coat in brilliant orange.

Missing words

round-necked	modelling
waist	t-shirt
boots	lining
tight	silver discs
layered	colours
sleeves	coat
floor-length	unisex

What to do

1 Work out where each of the missing words should go.
2 Work out the name of each of the models on the catwalk.
3 Make up a commentary for the two models and costumes which are not described.

Everybody else does it

Life was awfully old-fashioned. Dad was old-fashioned, he only did old-fashioned things like coming home from work and reading a newspaper, or watching television. Mum was old-fashioned, she only wore old-fashioned clothes, and old fashioned shoes. We lived in an old-fashioned house, decorated with old-fashioned furniture. I was brought up in an old-fashioned way imprisoned in an old-fashioned bedroom. There was plenty of fashionable life going on in the outside world, but I hadn't discovered it until I was sixteen.

When I was sixteen, I left school, needless to say, so I could be fashionable. My life really changed for the best. I found a job, made plenty of friends, bought plenty of fashionable clothes, and cosmetics and things for my room. I went to lots of places, such as dance clubs, discothèques, theatres and parties. Then, I met Nicky. Nicky and I had met when I was seventeen. He was at a get-together party I went to, and just by taking one look at him, I could tell he was really fashionable. When he asked me to dance, that was it really.

We, Nicky and I that is, decided to go steady. We weren't in love, but people said we made a good pair as we were both extremely fashionable, and we had a modern outlook on life, and going together brought us closer to each other. One day, it happened. Nicky proposed to me. I told him at first how terribly old-fashioned getting married would be. He said he didn't care, that he loved me and that was all that mattered. 'OK Nicky,' I told him, 'but you'll have to meet my parents.' He agreed, and I took him home.

'Mum, this is Nicky.' Mum stared at Nicky as if he had just popped out of her nightmares. 'Mum, Nicky's my boy-friend.'

'How d'you do,' Nicky said, stepping forward, greeting Mum in the old-fashioned way. Mum said nothing.

'Mum,' I said angrily, 'Nicky and I are going to get engaged.' That was it really, Mum just seemed to crack.

'Over my dead body!' she said as she wiped her hands dry on her apron. Then with a waving finger and a fierce expression Mum said, 'You're only doing it because you think that's what everybody else does.'

'That's right Mum. Everybody else does it so why can't I?'

'OK . . .' Mum said, 'you do it, but don't come back here.'

Nicky was silent, and didn't speak until we were outside. 'Terribly old-fashioned, isn't she!' he exclaimed.

'Yes,' I said, and although Nicky didn't know, I had made up my mind to collect my things and move into his flat, with him.

When I had told Nicky my idea, he seemed pleased by it.

'But there's only one thing,' Nicky said.

'What?' I gasped, as my mind raced to the thought that he was probably living with another girl.

'If you move in with me, that means we can't get engaged, because we will be using extra resources, and the bills will be increased.'

'Oh Nicky, I'll pay half,' I declared. 'We'll side it.' I don't know what it was, but Nicky didn't seem too pleased on our plans about getting engaged. 'Is it my mother?' I asked. He nodded, but I still moved in with him.

When I was leaving home, Mum began to warn me against the danger of the outside world. I told her how awfully old-fashioned I thought she and Dad had been.

'And when you get into any trouble,' Mum said, 'don't come to us.' Then I left.

Living with Nicky was like heaven. We both went out to work to pay our bills, and the rent. I could go wherever I pleased, and come home whatever time I wanted, providing I went with Nicky. Then I realised that Nicky had become possessive over me. If I spoke to a guy in a bar, he went wild with anger, saying I should never speak to other guys, yet he was free to chat to any girl; I didn't say anything. Nicky began to say that I should be indoors to serve his lunch, that if we were going to get married I might as well start practising. I reminded him that he was being very unbearably old-fashioned, and it later came to the point when I had to tell him that if he was going to be old-fashioned, then I may as well go back to Mum and Dad.

Despite what they had been through with me trying to be fashionable, Mum and Dad took me back. Thinking I had merely lived and learnt, Mum gave me a shoulder to cry on. I told her how unhappy I was during my short stay with Nicky, and I even confessed to how foolish I had been.

'You're still only young,' Mum said reassuringly, 'you're still my little baby. And when you're ready, you'll find a nice young man.'

I listened to Mum's words, and I cried. She knew I would never want to see Nicky again as we were not compatible; but what she didn't know, was that her 'little baby' was pregnant.

Stella Ibekwe   from *More to life than Mr Right* ed. R. Stokes

RULES

1 The game is played by any number

2 The object of the game is to be the *game of life*. You do this by collec... winner is the first player to collect

3 At the beginning of play, each play... it on the START square. The *Luck...* are shuffled and placed on the boar...

4 Play begins by each player throwin... The player who throws the highest...

5 When it is your turn, you throw the... that number of squares forward. T... instructions on the square you land...

6 Every time you pass the START squ... *token*.

The game

Some people say that life is like a game of luck. This board game is based on that idea. The game is incomplete: we can only see some of the squares, part of the rules and none of the cards.

1   Think about what should go on the missing squares and also what number 40, the finishing square, should be. Make a list of squares, starting with 1 and going on to 40.

2   There are two kinds of 'luck' card: **Disasters** and **Lucky Breaks**. What kind of good luck should be on the **Lucky Breaks** cards? Make up a series of lucky breaks to go on them.

3   Now do the same for the **Disasters** cards.

4   Copy out and complete the rules. Add any extra rules you think are needed.

Real life

Of course, real life isn't a game. We don't throw a dice to find out what's going to happen to us, nor do we draw cards. Even so, most people have got advantages and disadvantages, good points and bad points, as they face their lives. Think about your own life and personality. Make two lists:

a) My advantages and good qualities.
b) How they might help me in the future.

Now make two more lists:
c) Advantages and good qualities I wish I had.
d) How they would help me.

My advantages and good qualities

Good at practical things, eg mending a puncture

I get on with most people, and make friends easily

I'm very fit and do lots of sport

How they might help me

Help me in DIY work and in learning a skill

Helpful when I leave work and have to mix with lots of different people

Help me to stay healthy

What kind of job?

When you are thinking about your future, you may be asked what **kind** of job you want to aim for. Jobs can be described in many different ways. For example:

General Service
Would you like to work with and for people, as opposed to making things? (But not just people in trouble – see 'Social Service'.)

Practical
Do you enjoy making and mending things?

Outdoor / Active
Does the idea of using your muscles and/or working outdoors appeal to you?

Scientific
Are you interested in how and why things work?

Social Service
Do you want to help people in trouble?

Persuading and influencing
Are you good at organising people? And getting them to do what you want?

Literary
Are you a good talker? Do you express yourself well in writing?

Artistic
Do you like making things and entertaining people? Or do you simply have a good eye?

Computational
Are you good at figure work?

Nature
Would you like to work with animals or plants?

Choosing

Which of these types of work interest you? Why?

General Service
1 *Indoor / less active* secretary, telephonist, computer operator
2 *Indoor / more active* swimming-pool attendant, hospital porter
3 *Outdoor / active* window-cleaner, traffic warden

Practical
4 *Engineering, building crafts, electronics* welder, carpenter
5 *Shops, repairs, arts and crafts* hairdresser, bicycle-repairer
6 *Factories* sewing-machinist, packer
7 *Outdoor / active* seaman, bus-driver

Outdoor/active
8 *Tough and dangerous* coal-miner, fisherman
9 *Hard physical work, sometimes in uncomfortable surroundings* car breaker, construction-worker
10 *Other* forecourt sales staff, motor cycle messenger

Juri Gabriel *Unqualified Success*

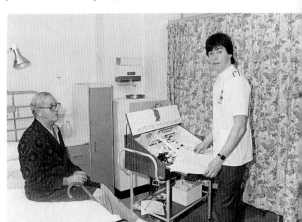

What goes where?

	Scientific	Social service	General service	Persuading influencing	Literary	Artistic	Computational	Practical	Outdoor active	Nature
Actor					■	■				
Air cabin crew		■	■	■			■		■	
Aircraft mechanic	■						■	■	■	
Antique dealer			■	■		■	■	■	■	
				■		■		■		

Which of the ten categories would you put each of these jobs into?

fireman	TV service engineer
bricklayer	shop assistant
travel agent	policeman / woman
postman	street market trader
plasterer	soldier

Many jobs fit into more than one category. Copy out the table in full. Put each of these jobs into the correct column(s):

coal-miner	electrician
forestry worker	glazier
holiday camp staff	jeweller
laundry-worker	nurse
plumber	milk roundsman

Looking at the job in detail

Choose a job that you know something about, for example, one that is done by a person you know well. Write a description of it, following the pattern in the example.

Holiday camp staff

Responsibilities and duties	Skills and abilities needed	For	Against
See that everything runs smoothly. Organise games, competitions, etc. Chat to people, jolly them along and sort out problems.	Fitness, energy. Smart appearance. Outgoing personality. Responsible, helpful, efficient, polite nature. Sense of humour.	Responsible, lively and rewarding work. Meet lots of people, and have a good time. May get reduced-price holidays.	Noisy, tiring and emotionally demanding. Irregular, unsocial and long hours. Seasonal work. Some people are unpleasant and complain a lot.

Preparing for work

EDDIE

<u>Best Subjects at school</u> : CDT, Geography, Chemistry.

<u>Main interests</u> : 'Motorbikes, supporting Spurs, playing football.'

LOUISE

<u>Best subjects at school</u> : English, French, Biology.

<u>Main interests</u> : 'Nothing really. I like listening to music and going around with my friends. I get bored when I'm on my own.'

MIRIAM

<u>Best subjects at school</u> : CDT, Maths, Games.

<u>Main interests</u> : 'I don't have time for much, because we're a large family, Mum is often ill, and I have to help out a lot at home.'

WAYNE

<u>Best subjects at school</u> : CDT, Maths, Games.

<u>Main interests</u> : 'Making and flying model aeroplanes, pop music, reading.'

The kind of job you can aim for depends on you: your personality, your interests, your work at school. Look at the case studies. Copy and complete this table. Think about each person. What kind of job do you think each one should aim for and why?

Name	Interests	Best subjects at school.

What is the employer looking for?

What the employer wants to know	Hobbies and activities that prove it
How well will you do the job? Are you	
1 Fit?	
2 Good with your hands?	Makes clothes, models, paintings or anything. Mends things.
3 Quick learner?	Can do a lot of different things.
4 Hard worker?	
Can you be relied on? Are you	
5 Punctual, polite, neat, clean, smart?	Employer will judge for him/herself at interview.
6 Honest?	Has handled money. (e.g. in Saturday job)
7 Responsible?	Has earned money, helps in house.

Completing the table

1 There are no activities suggested for **Hard worker** and **Fit**. Can you think of activities that should go in these spaces?

2 These phrases have been missed out from the table. Where should they go?

1) Helps decorate the house.

2) Is good at cooking, sewing, music, a hobby – anything that needs time and effort.

3) Babysits, helps in house, looks after animals or garden.

4) Cooks, gardens, cuts hair, etc.

5) Does a newspaper round.

6) Is in charge of something at school.

Leaving School

This is the beginning of a story about people leaving school. The passage has been divided into eleven sections. Number 1 is printed at the beginning, and number 11 is printed at the end. The others have been jumbled up. Read them through and work out the order in which they should be read.

1 Sean Tinnersley didn't know exactly what he was expecting, but whatever it was, it didn't happen. For the last ten minutes of the last 'lesson' he couldn't keep his eyes off his watch. Mr Dyer (of Dyer here fame) kept rubbishing on, but no one, just nobody, was listening. The noise level was fantastic, and Sean had a pretty fair idea that it was the same all over their floor. Who wanted to hear about the great big outside world from Dyer, anyhow? In ten minutes time they'd be out in it. For good.

2 The three of them exchanged a glance. Sammy thought that Mr Parks was being a miserable prat, but they didn't want a fight. That would be stupid.

'Sorry,' he said, for Roger.

3 A few staff hung about, their backs pressed to the walls, smiling weakly, and shouting out farewells to the kids they liked. A couple of the nastier ones pushed through the sea of pupils like sharks, with cutting faces on. Sean and Sammy stood at the bottom of the stairway and watched them all.

4 'Don't give me that,' said Roger, with a grin. 'You'll be back, Tinnersley, you can't leave it alone. You'll get two dozen O-levels and you'll be down that sixth form college like a shot. It's me and Sammy who'll be out, mate. On our own.'

Mr Dyer was winding up: 'So anyway, men,' he said, 'I really do wish you all the very—'

The school bell clicked, which meant it was about to go off like a thing demented.

5   They laughed as they struggled through the door.

   'Talking of which,' said Roger, 'I'm going for a pee. See you down the bottom of the stairs, all right?'

   The area behind the main glass doors was chaos. All the leavers were milling around in droves, screeching and whooping at each other.

6   'It's funny, Sam,' said Sean. 'It's the last time, d'you realise that? We'll never have to do all this again.'

   'Yeah,' said Sammy. 'It's like being let out of clink, innit? We ought to go and have a good old nosh up, at Alec's caff, like prisoners do on the films.'

   'But do you *feel* anything?' asked Sean. 'I mean, it seems to –'

7   A cheer went up, which drowned out Dyer – and the bell – totally. It turned into a chant:

   'Dyer here, Dyer here, Dyer'ere, Dyer'ere, Diarrhoea!'

   Mr Dyer smiled broadly, and raised his hands for silence after a couple of minutes.

   'Thanks lads,' he said. 'I think that just about sums you up! Best of luck. The very best of luck!'

   There was another cheer, with some kind of affection in it. In the crush to leave the room Sammy ended up jammed in with them.

8   He glanced at his watch. Eight minutes. Seven and a half. It was the last lesson of the last day of the last term of the last year. Of the lot. They were on their way.

   He nudged Roger, who was lounging next to him, about to flick a lump of dead chewing gum across the room at Sammy, their mate.

   'Hey,' he said. 'This is it, Rog. In five minutes time we're free. "I will kiss the Sergeant Major, no more lousy school for me"'!

9   Roger Unsworth interrupted the thought, by sliding down the banister and arriving between them like a ton of bricks. The caretaker, one of the roaming sharks, homed in on him hungrily, nostrils dilated with the smell of blood.

   'Oy,' he said unpleasantly. 'Oy you. Cut out acting like a hooligan, get it?'

10   'He's a good bloke, that Dyer,' he said. 'What do you think, Rog?'

   'Yeah,' said Roger. 'Wonderful. But he didn't teach you much, did he, Sam? 'Cept how to enjoy a good skive at the back.'

   Sammy smiled through his powerful round glasses.

   'That's because I'm workshy, Rog. The careers master says so. You can't blame Diarrhoea for that, now can you!'

11   'Sorry?' said Mr Parks. 'Sorry ain't going to do any good when I've got to scrape this idiot up off the floor, now is it?'

   Sean and Sammy put on their humble schoolboy look, prepared to shamble off. But Roger gave an insolent grin.

Jan Needle *Going Out*

Question

What do you think Roger did and/or said? Tell the story of what happened next.

A woman's place

Look at the picture strip opposite.

Pair conversations

1 Choose one of these conversation starters.
2 Decide who the two characters are.
3 Decide who will be each character.
4 Decide when and where the conversation takes place.
5 Act out the conversation making it up as you go along.

One

A: I've had enough of this.
B: What's the matter?
A: I've worked my fingers to the bone all day and all you do when you come home is lounge around the place.

Two

A: You're looking a bit fed up.
B: 'Fed up?' That's putting it mildly.
A: What is it?
B: It's that husband of mine. He never does a stroke of work.

Writing

1 Choose one of the conversation starters. Write the whole conversation as a script.
2 The husband is on holiday from work and his wife is suddenly taken ill. He has to do all the jobs you see opposite. At the end of a long day, when the children are asleep and his wife is settled down for the night, he is able to put his feet up. You are the husband. Write down your thoughts as you look back on the day's events.

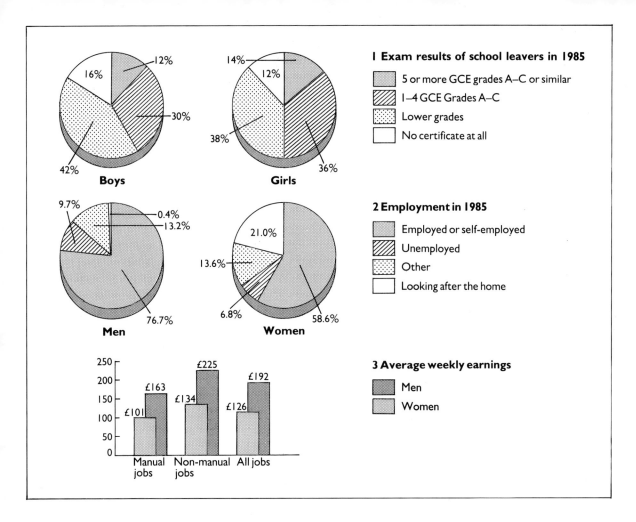

1 Exam results of school leavers in 1985

- 5 or more GCE grades A–C or similar
- 1–4 GCE Grades A–C
- Lower grades
- No certificate at all

Boys: 12%, 30%, 42%, 16%

Girls: 14%, 12%, 36%, 38%

2 Employment in 1985

- Employed or self-employed
- Unemployed
- Other
- Looking after the home

Men: 0.4%, 13.2%, 9.7%, 76.7%

Women: 21.0%, 13.6%, 6.8%, 58.6%

3 Average weekly earnings

- Men
- Women

Manual jobs: £101, £163
Non-manual jobs: £134, £225
All jobs: £126, £192

Women and work

Although things have changed, many women still think that we live in an unequal society.

Questions

1 **On average** do boys or girls leave school with better qualifications?
2 If a man and a woman work full-time, who is likely to earn more?
3 How do most women spend their time?

Discussion points

1 Look at your answers to questions 1–3. What is your opinion of this situation?
2 What do you think of each of these opinions?
  a) There's no point in spending money educating girls as much as boys. They're only going to end up married and having children.
  b) Just being a housewife is a waste of most women's talents.
  c) Housewives should be paid for the work they do.
  d) **All** household chores should be equally divided between husband and wife.

Women talking

Three poems for women

1   This is a poem for a woman doing dishes.
    This is a poem for a woman doing dishes.
    It must be repeated.
    It must be repeated,
    again and again,
    again and again.
    because the woman doing dishes
    because the woman doing dishes
    has trouble hearing
    has trouble hearing.

2   And this is another poem for a woman
    cleaning the floor
    who cannot hear at all.
    Let us have a moment for silence
    for the woman who cleans the floor.

3   And here is one more poem
    for the woman at home
    with children.
    You never see her at night.
    Stare at an empty space and imagine her there,
    the woman with children
    because she cannot be here to speak
    for herself,
    and listen
    to what you think
    she might say.

Susan Griffin

Rose Schlosinger was born in 1907. Arrested by the Nazis in Germany on 18 September 1942, because she belonged to a resistance group, she was executed on 5 August 1943. Her husband Bodo, an interpreter with the German military police, ended his life by shooting himself in a Russian farmhouse when he learned that his wife had been condemned to death.

Rose wrote this letter to her young daughter, Marianne, the day she was executed.

5 August 1943

My dear little big Marianne,

I do not know when you will read this letter. I leave it to Granny or Daddy to give to you when you are old enough for it. Now I must say farewell to you, because we shall probably never see each other again.

Nevertheless, you must grow up to be a healthy, happy and strong human being. I hope that you will experience the most beautiful things the world has to give, as I have, without having to undergo its hardships, as I have had to do. First of all, you must strive to become capable and industrious, then all the other happiness will come of itself. Do not be too prodigal of your feelings. There are not many men who are like Daddy, as good and pure in their love. Learn to wait before giving all your love – thus you will be spared the feeling of having been cheated. But a man who loves you so much that he will share all the suffering and all difficulties with you, and for whom you can do the same – such a man you may love, and believe me, the happiness you will find with him will repay you for the waiting.

I wish you a great many years of happiness that I unfortunately could have for only a few. And then you must have children: when they put your first child into your arms, perhaps you will think of me – that it was a high moment in my life too when for the first time I held you, a little red bundle, in my arms. And then think of our evenings of discussion in bed, about all the important things of life – I trying to answer your questions. And think of our beautiful three weeks at the seashore – of the sunrise, and when we walked barefoot along the beach from Bansin to Uckeritz, and when I pushed you before me on the rubber float, and when we read books together. We had so many beautiful things together, my child, and you must experience all of them over again, and much more besides.

And there is still another thing I want to tell you. When we must die, we are sorry for every unkind word we have said to someone who is dear to us; if we could go on living, we should remember that and control ourselves much better. Perhaps you can remember it; you would make life – and later on death too – easier for yourself and for others.

And be happy, as often as you can – every day is precious. It is a pity about every minute that one has spent in sadness.

My love for you shall accompany you your whole life long. I kiss you – and all who are kind to you. Farewell, my dear – thinking of you to the end with the greatest love.

Your Mother

Summer holiday job

One of the Summer Schools is going to take place in your area.
'Family guides' of your age will be needed to help run it.
This Special is about how these people
are recruited.

Anglo-American Summer Schools

This summer American High School students have the opportunity for an entirely new educational experience. How would **you** like to visit Great Britain, see the sights that made Old England famous and live as the guest of a British family?

Lectures and discussions will be led by qualified British and American High School teachers and College lecturers. All afternoon trips will be accompanied by qualified adults.

Course members will be divided into 'families' — small groups of 4 or 5. Each family will have a British High School student of the same age to accompany it throughout the course. These 'family guides' are currently being recruited in British schools. They will be fully trained in readiness for the Summer Schools.

This year we are running Summer Schools at five centers in different parts of Britain. The program at each center will vary slightly, but the basic pattern is the same at all of them:
Morning: a program of lectures, films and discussions about the British way of life.
Afternoon: coach trips and rail visits to places of interest in the region.
Evening: usually free, although some special events are planned.

Discussion points

1 What personal qualities would the family guides need?
2 Would they need any special qualifications or knowledge? Remember that they will be trained for the work.
3 They will have to work every afternoon from 2pm until 6pm and on two or three evenings a week. How much do you think they should be paid?

Making up an advert

You are one of the British organisers. You have to make up an advertisement, inviting young people to apply for one of these family guide jobs.

Information

Period involved: 25 July–15 August
Advertisement being issued by:
    Harold Treadwell
    Anglo-American Summer Schools
    Verity House
    Clarkson Street
    Birdwell
    SA12 5TG

You are going to make up an advertisement either for a local newspaper, or for local radio.

1 Decide on these points:
    a) the kind of person you want to attract.
    b) how to make the job sound attractive to them.
    c) the information they need about the summer school. This should include times and places, and should be based on your local area.
    d) the details of how they should apply.
2 Now make up your advert.

Applying

Talented young people wanted

and 17

g and

d?

g with young Ame

al atmosphere?

IF SO and you would like further information and an
application form, contact:

Harold Treadwell
Anglo-American Summer Schools
Verity House
Clarkson Street
Birdwell
SA12 5TG
or telephone Suzanne Wood or James Merton on
0321 9832

Answering by phone

For this exercise you need to work with a partner.

1 Decide who is:
   A the applicant
   B Suzanne Wood, or James Merton.
2 Think carefully about what you are going to say.
3 Sit back-to-back.
4 Begin with B answering the phone.

Answering by letter

Write a letter to Mr Treadwell, asking him for further information and an application form. If you are not sure how to set the letter out, look at pages 118–121.

1 Copy out the form and fill it in.
2 Write the letter to go with it.

APPLICATION FORM

Surname _____

First names _____

Date of birth _____

Name of parents or legal guardians _____ Age _____

Address _____

Home telephone number _____

School at present attended _____

Name of Headmaster _____

Name and address of one other person who will support your application _____

NOTES

You should accompany this form with the following:
1 A statement signed by parents or legal guardians, giving their consent for you to apply.
2 A letter explaining why you want this job and why you think you are suitable for it.
3 A recent photograph.

Selection

65, Rackham Road,
Benson
Shropshire
SH6 8YG

Dear Mr Tredwll,
    I wish to aply for one of the jobs you are adverticing.
I would like a holiday job.
I think I could do this job well.
          your sincerly
              E. A. Houlden

29, Outer Ring Road,
Oxford,
OX9 4GR
10th April 1987

Dear Mr Treadwell,
    I have just been told about your advertisement by a friend who lives in Stafford. Although I don't live in Burdwell, or anywhere near it, I know it quite well. This is because my grandmother lives there, and I often visit her during the school holidays. This Summer I am due to spend the whole of the summer holiday with her. I know that Gran is going to find it a bit of a strain having me for six weeks, so if I could get a job, it would help a lot. I like mixing with new people and enjoy going on trips and visits. I am sure that I could soon pick up what I don't know about the area. I do hope that you will be able to give me this opportunity.
          Yours sincerely,

              Anne Grant.

32, Redwood Lane,
Churcham
Staffs
ST21 6th
21st April 1988

Dear Mr Treadwell,
    I wish to apply for a holiday job with the Anglo-American Summer School this year. I enclose an application form and a letter from my parents.
    I should like this job because I like meeting new people. I would find it particulary interesting to meet American students because I have an American penfriend and I write to her regularly. One day I hope to be able to go to America and meet her.
    I have lived in Churcham since I was seven, so I know the area very well. I think I find it easy to get on with people, so I shouldn't find it too difficult to fit in with the course students. I hope that you are able to give me one of these jobs.
          Yours Sincerely,

              Hilary Stephens.

43 Amersham Drive
Thurs 14th April

Dear Sir or madame
I would like one of those holiday
jobs and hope you can give me
one. I think I've got a lot to offer and
I reckon I work hard, so you wouldn't
be making a mistake with me. I know
the old town pretty well and I'd
be able to show your students to
one or two places other people don't
know about! I've got a bit of a
sense of humor and I like meeting
people. I think that's very important
when you're dealing with people, don't
you? So please give me an interview
Yours faithfully
   Arthur James.

The interview

This exercise needs to be done in groups of three or four:

    A first interviewer
    B second interviewer
    C first applicant
    D second applicant

If there are only three in the group, miss out B.

What to do

1. Choose the applicants from the letters on these pages.
2. Decide who is playing each part.
3. Spend some time thinking about your character and how s/he will tackle the interview.
4. Decide on the order in which the interviews will happen.
5. Set up a table or desk and chairs.
6. When everyone is ready start the first interview.
7. At the end, the interviewer(s) should decide on **one** person who has got the job, and explain why.

Making a shortlist

You are going to interview people applying for the holiday jobs. You have to choose two from the four letters.

1. Read them all carefully.
2. Try to work out the kind of person who wrote each one.
3. How suitable would each one be?
4. Write a short report on each applicant. Include:
   a) Your impressions of his or her personality.
   b) Whether you think s/he is likely to be suitable.
5. Decide which two you would interview and why.

Planning and drafting

Writing is a good way of...finding out what you know and think
discovering new things
sorting out your ideas
recording what you know and think
communicating with other people.
It's difficult to do all these things at the same time.

Finding out what you know and think

When you are preparing to write about a subject, for example, local newspapers, there are several ways of finding out what you know and think.

Making a list

Just write down all the thoughts that come into your head. Don't worry about how they fit together, just write down everything.

Reporters   Circulation
Features   Popularity
Adverts   Competitions

Making a web

Draw a diagram like this, with the subject in the middle.

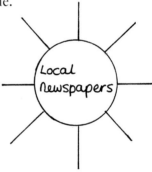

At the end of each line put one idea.
Then try to split up each of these ideas into more ideas.

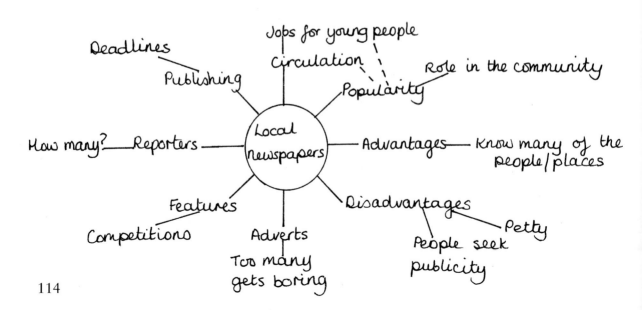

114

What you know and what you don't know

Make two lists: one of the things that you do know about the subject, and one of things you need to find out.

<u>Things I know</u>

Circulation
Popularity
Advantages
Disadvantages
Adverts

<u>Things I need to find out</u>

Reporters?
Publishing?
Interviews?
Features?
News - worldwide?
Deadlines

Discovering new things

There are many ways in which you can find out new information and ideas:
Radio
TV
Newspapers
Magazines
Encyclopaedias and other books
Teletext: Oracle and Ceefax
Prestel and other viewdata systems
Asking people: friends
                 family
                 teachers
                 librarians
                 experts
Writing for information
Going to the library:
                 look on the shelves
                 use the catalogue
                 go to the reference section
                 ask a librarian to help you

Sorting out ideas and information

When you have collected information and ideas, you need to put them into an order that makes sense.

This is one way of doing it.

1   Read **everything** you have written so far.
2   Think about it all. Try to decide what is most important and why.
3   Make a list of the most important points.

    1 Reporters
    2 Publishing
    3 Contents
    4 Deadlines
    5 Popularity
    6 Advantages
    7 Disadvantages
    8 Circulation

4   Decide what is the best order in which to write about them.

    1 Circulation
    2 Popularity
    3 Reporters
    4 Publishing
    5 Deadlines
    6 Advantages
    7 Disadvantages
    8 Contents

5   Write a **first draft.** Don't worry if it doesn't follow your list exactly. You will probably find that you think of new ideas as you write.

The circulation of the newspaper is important to its life and its role in the community. The people who deliver our newspapers work in all weathers so the newspaper depends on them, as much as people buying the paper because without them we wouldn't have our local paper. To keep going the newspaper has to sell a certain amount of copies so that the reporters have to make the paper look good with pictures and articles, that the general public enjoy. The reporter's job is very tough because if they didn't do a good job not many people would buy the paper and so we wouldn't have a paper. Survival of a newspaper therefore depends on the skills of the reporters and editorial staff.

Writing a final version

A first draft isn't the same as a final version. Very few people can write something and get it right first time. Your writing needs to be revised so that:

- it says exactly what you want it to say,
- other people can understand it easily,
- it doesn't contain a lot of mistakes.

Here are some ideas:

1   When you have finished writing, read through what you have written. Change the parts you don't like.

2   Even better, when you have finished, put the writing away. Come back to it after a time and **then** revise it.

3   Ask someone else to read it and comment on it:
      a friend
      someone in the family
      a teacher.

> The circulation of the newspaper is important to its life and its role in the community. The people who deliver our newspapers work in all weathers so the newspaper depends on them, as much as people buying the paper because without them we wouldn't have our local paper. To keep going the newspaper has to sell a certain ~~amount~~ number of copies so that the reporters have to make the paper ~~look good~~ attractive with pictures and articles, that the general public enjoy. The ~~reporter's job is very tough because if they didn't do a good job not many people would buy the paper and so we wouldn't have a paper.~~ Survival of a newspaper therefore depends on the skills of the reporters and editorial staff.

4   When you are finally satisfied with it, you can write a neat final version.

> The circulation of the newspaper is important to its life and its role in the community. The people who deliver our newspapers work in all weathers so the newspaper depends on them, as much as people buying the paper, because without them we wouldn't have our local paper. To keep going a newspaper has to sell a certain number of copies so the reporters have to make the paper attractive with pictures and articles that the general public enjoy. The survival of a newspaper therefore depends on the skills of the reporters and editorial staff.

Letters

Bev
Called but you were out. I'm free next week. Can we meet then to go flat hunting?

love Delroy

Midshires Electricity Board
Monterey Street
Flaxby
Lincs

To: The Occupier
Flat 8 Sinclair Mansions
Flaxby   Date as postmark

Dear Sir/Madam

The electricity supply to the above property was disconnected on ..10.7.88.. If you wish to have it reconnected you should apply in person to the office named at the top of this letter. There will/~~will not~~ be a reconnection charge of £.22.50...

Yours faithfully

for E. F. Hargreaves
District Manager

Write or phone?

People sometimes say that nowadays you don't need to write letters. It's quicker and easier to use the phone. Look at the four letters. Why didn't the writers of these letters use the phone instead?

Formal or informal?

How you write a letter depends on why you are writing it and how well you know the person you are writing to. Copy and complete this table.

If you . . .	Begin with . . .	End with . . .
		Yours faithfully,
	Dear Mr/Mrs/Ms	
know the person well		

19, Mandarin Road
Flaxby.
Lincs
Friday 15th July

Dear Delroy, It was great to hear from you!
I wish Dad would change his mind and
let us go on the 'phone. I've decided that
the best thing to do is to meet at the
Bridge Café at half past 8 next Tuesday
morning. Then we can have the whole day
for flat hunting. We just _must_ find somewhere
for Louise to live – it's only ten days now
before she arrives.

See ya!

Ben

Orange Tree Properties
Wilmott Street
Flaxby
Lincs L12 9FZ

Ms B. Roberts
19 Mandarin Road
Flaxby
Lincs

23rd July 1988

Dear Ms Roberts,

Flat 8, Sinclair Mansions, Flaxby

Thank you for telephoning
yesterday. I wish to confirm
receipt of your deposit for rent
on this property. It will be
available for your sister to
occupy from 1st August 1988. The
terms and conditions are set down
in the enclosed documents.

Yours sincerely,

Harold J. Barstow

What are the rules?

Look at the letters, and at the table.
Now explain what you think the rules are.
Do it by copying and completing these
sentences, but add extra sentences as needed.

If you know the person well _____
If you have met the person, but do not
know him or her well _____
If you have never met or spoken to the
person _____

FARNSWORTH BROS
FIRST CLASS SKIP SERVICE
FOR
SCRAP & WASTE
FACTORY CONTRACTS
HIGHEST CASH BUYERS
FOR ALL SCRAP METAL

EXTON OLD COLLIERY
DEANSWORTH
NOTTINGHAM
(0623) 3917

37, Burton Lane
Kyneton,
Notts

30 April 1988

Dear Sir,

I'd like to know more about the scrap metal business.

Yours faithfully,

P L Hammerton

Exercise

1. There is one major difference in the way the two letters are set out. What is it?
2. This is a diagram of how the first letter is set out. Draw a similar diagram to show how the second letter is set out.

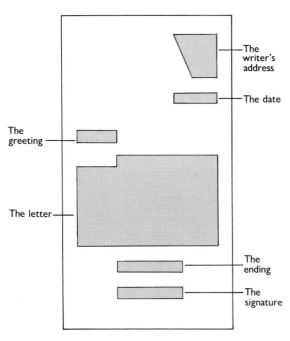

- The writer's address
- The date
- The greeting
- The letter
- The ending
- The signature

3. Write a reply to Mr Farnsworth's letter, explaining that you are doing a project on waste and recycling. You want to find out more about how the scrap metal business works.

FARNSWORTH BROS

Scrap Metal Merchants

Exton Old Collierty
Deansworth
Nottingham

Mr P. L. Hammerton,
37, Burton Lane,
Kyneton,
Notts.   10th May 1988

Dear Mr Hammerton,

Thank you for your letter. It is a bit difficult to answer as it stands. Could you tell us more clearly what it is you want to know? For example, are you interested in trying to get a job in scrap metal? If you will explain exactly what information you are looking for, we will try to help you.

Yours faithfully

pp J. Farnsworth

The HOUSEMARTINS

Early in 1984, after a year spent travelling around Europe, singer Paul Heaton arrives to live in Hull. Sensing that great musical revolutions might as well start off from humble fishing ports instead of vast media capitals, Paul places a postcard in his front window. The postcard requests similarly interested young musicians to get in touch to see about setting up a band. Seven doors away down the same street lives Stan Cullimore. Owning a guitar and a voice, he calls in to see Paul. The next six months find the pair rehearsing, writing material and performing as the first incarnation of the Housemartins.

Drummer Hugh Whitaker and original bassist, Ted Kay, are recruited from fellow Hull band The Gargoyles to flesh out the live and recorded sound of the Housemartins, and everyone reels in amazement upon the discovery that both new members own fine singing voices in addition to their skills in the rhythm department. The arrangement soon becomes a permanent one and, flying under the self-proclaimed banner of 'The Housemartins are Quite Good', the band continue writing, rehearsing and gigging. Their now highly distinctive four-part vocal harmonies are often heard to best effect on the note-perfect a cappella numbers with which the Housemartins pepper their live set, taking gospel classics and turning young British audiences into swooning congregations.

105

COREY HART
c/o EMI Records
6920 Sunset Boulevard
Los Angeles
California 90028
USA

also

c/o EMI Records
1370 Avenue of the
Americas
New York
NY 10019
USA

also

'Shades'
6265 Cote De Liesse
St Laurent
Quebec
Canada H42 IC3

HAWKWIND
29 Corden Street
Wisbech
Cambridgeshire
TE13 2LW
England

HEAVEN 17
c/o Virgin Records
(Press Office)
Kensal House
553–579 Harrow Road
London W10
England

**FINIS
HENDERSON**
c/o Motown Records
Corporation
6255 Sunset Boulevard
Los Angeles
California 90028
USA

JIMI HENDRIX
76 Mill Road
Royston
Hertfordshire
England

NICK HEYWARD
c/o Arista Records
(Press Office)
3 Cavendish Square
London W1M 9HA
England

HI-TENSION
c/o Street Wave Records
3–4 Queens Drive
West Acton
London W3
England

JOOLS HOLLAND
7 Hassenden Road
Blackheath
London SE3
England

**HOT CHOCOLATE
(ERROL BROWN)**
c/o WEA
(Press Office)
20 Broadwick Street
London W1V 2DJ
England

**THE
HOUSEMARTINS**
173 Newlands Avenue
Hull HU5 2EP
England

**WHITNEY
HOUSTON**
c/o Arista Records
(Press Office)
3 Cavendish Square
London W1M 9HA
England

HUMAN LEAGUE
c/o Virgin Records
(Press Office)
Kensal House
553–579 Harrow Road
London W10
England

ICICLE WORKS
Electric Ice
PO Box 162
Liverpool L69 2LH
England

25

Writing to find out

Choose one of the groups or performers listed on this page. Write a letter asking for information about them and their fan club.

Punctuation

Capital letters

Capital letters are used:

1. To begin a sentence.
2. For the word **I**.
   Yesterday **I** went to school.
3. For the main words in titles.
4. For days and months.
   On Thursday March 23rd I went to see *Son of Rambo* at the cinema.
5. For people's names and titles.
6. For initials.
   My grandfather is **Mr Henry J**. Peabody Junior.

Full stops

Full stops are used:

1. To end a sentence.
   This is the end of the sentence.

2. After initials.
   Mr G.R.B. Hanson

3. After abbreviations.
   Mr G.R.B.Hanson, M.C., M.P.

Exceptions

Full stops are not used after these abbreviations:

1. Mr Mrs Dr Revd Mme Mlle
2. Well-known organisations, such as BBC ITV

Commas

Commas are used:

1. To separate the different things in a list.

   For maths lessons you will need a ruler, a pencil, a pair of compasses, a protractor, and a calculator.

2. To make the meaning of a sentence clear by separating groups of words. There are two important rules.

   a) Do I need a pause when I am reading it?
   Even though I know you weren't in the room at the time, I still think you had something to do with the explosion.
   b) Is the sentence confusing if I don't have a comma in it?
   If you don't stop shaking, the policeman will think you did it.

3. In direct speech. See page 125.

Colons

Colons are used:
1. To introduce a list.

   For this field trip, you will need the following outdoor clothing: thick sweater, jeans, strong boots, anorak.

2. To introduce a saying, statement, or idea.

   There was one thing she really cared about: the family must be kept together.

Apostrophes

Apostrophes are used:

1 To show where letters have been missed out:

    we are → we're
    are not → aren't
    he is   → he's
    I would → I'd

2 To show that something belongs to somebody:

    Whose bike is that? It is Paramjit's bike.

Rules

1 If the word ends in -s, just add an apostrophe:

    In our class the girls' exam marks are always better than the boys' results.

2 If the word does not end in -s, then add 's:

    I've got a brother and a sister: my sister's bedroom is always tidier than my brother's.

Special rules

1 **it is** becomes **it's**
   of it becomes **its**
2 **who's** means **who is**
   of whom becomes **whose**
3 **yours** not **your's**
   hers not **her's**
   theirs not **their's**
   ours not **our's**

Exercises

Write out the paragraphs that follow, adding all the necessary punctuation.

A I don't really know how the accident happened I'm usually so careful when I'm out on my own especially when it's getting dark on this occasion my mother had asked me to go and get some bread from the shop on the corner as it was beginning to get dark I made sure that my dynamo was working and that both lights went on I went down to the shop giving good hand signals when I turned right into the forecourt I bought the bread and put it into my saddlebag I turned out into the road very carefully and started for home there was hardly any traffic I don't know how it can have happened but somehow I didn't concentrate on what I was doing I think something must have caught my eye so that I didn't look where I was going the next thing I knew was a terrible crash and I was lying in the road with my bike tangled up in the rear bumper of an expensive sports car

B the bike was a dare not by anyone else because he was alone but a dare to himself the day had been draggy at school he had drifted from lesson to lesson half paying attention at first but gradually losing interest and spending most of the day doodling or signing his name eventually four oclock had arrived and hed gone back home hed enjoyed the walk because the weather was bright and sunny although there was a real winter snap about it

at home hed eaten tea then gone to his room and tried to do some work but somehow he just couldnt concentrate hed played some music but after one side of some heavy rock hed looked at his other records and just couldnt choose what to play he seemed to know them all so well and he wished he could buy something new

Nigel Hinton *Collision Course*

123

Writing speech

We can tell this story in three different forms:

    as a report
    as a script
    as direct speech.

Report

In a report we don't tell the exact words that were used, but we explain the gist of what was said.

I took Nicky round to meet my mum. When I told her that we wanted to get engaged she was furious. She told me that if we got engaged she'd never let me in the house again.

Script

Script is the form used in plays. Three different things have to be written down: The name of each speaker.
The exact words spoken.
Instructions for the actors. How to say the words and what to do.

Names of characters are in capital letters.
Always start a new line for new character speaking.)

After the name of the character put a colon.

Each speech starts at the same point on the line.

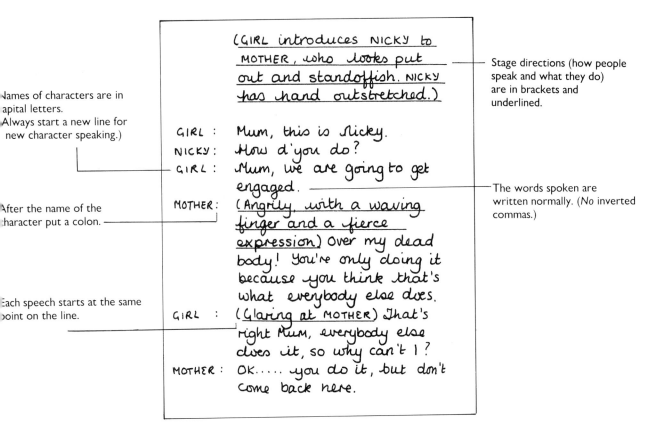

(GIRL introduces NICKY to MOTHER, who looks put out and standoffish. NICKY has hand outstretched.)

GIRL : Mum, this is Nicky.
NICKY : How d'you do?
GIRL : Mum, we are going to get engaged.
MOTHER : (Angrily, with a waving finger and a fierce expression) Over my dead body! You're only doing it because you think that's what everybody else does.
GIRL : (Glaring at MOTHER) That's right Mum, everybody else does it, so why can't I ?
MOTHER : OK..... you do it, but don't come back here.

Stage directions (how people speak and what they do) are in brackets and underlined.

The words spoken are written normally. (*No inverted commas.*)

Direct speech

Direct speech is used in stories.

Before the first inverted commas you must have either a comma (,) or a colon (:).

When a new person begins speaking, start a new line and go in a bit – this is called *indenting*.

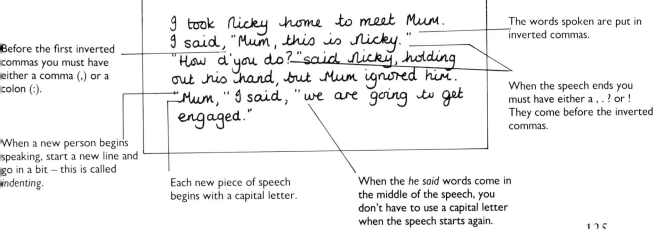

I took Nicky home to meet Mum. I said, "Mum, this is Nicky."
"How d'you do?" said Nicky, holding out his hand, but Mum ignored him.
"Mum," I said, "we are going to get engaged."

The words spoken are put in inverted commas.

When the speech ends you must have either a , . ? or ! They come before the inverted commas.

Each new piece of speech begins with a capital letter.

When the *he said* words come in the middle of the speech, you don't have to use a capital letter when the speech starts again.

125

Word study

unhappy, unlucky, unfortunate, despairing, hopeless, doomed, pitiable, poor, wretched, miserable, sad, melancholy, despondent, disconsolate, cut up, broken-hearted, sorrowful, weepy, tearful, in tears, disappointed, discontented, weary, fed up to the back teeth, bored, dejected, bitter, cross, sulky, pouting, sullen, grouchy, grumbling, grousing, whining, gloomy, downbeat, pessimistic, despairing, discouraged, disheartened, dismayed, troubled, worried, downcast, downhearted, droopy, low down, down in the mouth, low-spirited, depressed, out of sorts, not oneself, out of spirits, listless, ready to cry, browned off, cheesed off, sick as a parrot

cheerful, cheery, happy, hearty, optimistic, smiling, sunny, bright, beaming, radiant, in high spirits, in a good humour, upbeat, hopeful, carefree, light-hearted, happy-go-lucky, bouncing, jaunty, perky, chirpy, chipper, spirited, sprightly, vivacious, full of beans, full of pep, bright-eyed and bushy-tailed, on the top of one's form, content, contented, satisfied, comfortable, pleased, without complaints, easygoing, unworried, chuffed, pleased as Punch, over the moon, on top of the world, amused, exhilarated, walking on air, overjoyed, jubilant, delighted, ecstatic

be good. **optimist** n.
optimistic adj. showing optimism, hopeful.
optimistically n.
optimum adj. best, most favourable. —n.

despite prep. in spite of.
despondent adj. in low spirits, dejected.
despondently adv., **despondency** n.
despot (**dess**-pot) n. a tyrant, a ruler who

be bad. **pessimist** n.
pessimistic adj. showing pessimism.
pessimistically adv.
pest n. **1.** a troublesome or annoying

nection between its parts.
disconsolate (dis-**kon**-sŏ-lăt) adj. unhappy at the loss of something, disappointed. **disconsolately** adv.
discontent n. dissatisfaction, lack of con-

used as a unit of measurement.
radiant adj. **1.** giving out rays of light. **2.** looking very bright and happy. **3.** transmitting heat by radiation, (of heat) transmitted in this way. **radiantly** adv., **radiance** n.
radiate v. **1.** to spread outwards

JP abbrev. Justice of the Peace.
jubilant adj. showing joy, rejoicing.
jubilation n. rejoicing.

depression. **melancholic** (mel-ăn-**kol**-ik) adj.
melancholy (**mel**-ăn-kŏl-i) n. **1.** mental depression, thoughtful sadness. **2.** an atmosphere of gloom. —adj. sad, gloomy, depressing.
mélange (may-**lahn**zh) n. a mixture.

wards this kind of behaviour.
exhilarated adj. very happy or lively.
exhilaration n.
exhort (ig-**zort**) v. to urge or advise ear-

ecru (**ay**-kroo) n. light fawn colour.
ecstatic (ik-**stat**-ik) adj. feeling intense delight., **ecstatically** adv.
ectoplasm n. **1.** the outer portion of the

Making word lists

Read the passage that follows. In it the words **happy** and **miserable** are both repeated.

By the time I got home I was feeling really miserable. I don't really know why I felt so miserable, but perhaps it was because Donna had been so happy. When I got home it didn't help to find that Marty was so happy she could hardly keep still.

'Why are you so happy?' I asked.

'Why are you looking so miserable?' she said.

1   Find at least six words that might be used to replace **happy**. Write them down as a word wheel like this:

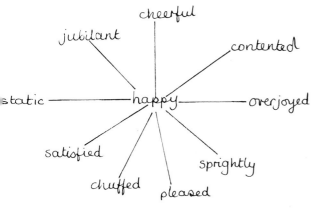

2   Now write them as a league table, with the strongest at the top and the weakest at the bottom, like this:

> ecstatic
> overjoyed
> jubilant
> chuffed
> sprightly
> cheerful
> pleased
> contented
> satisfied

3   Do a word wheel and a league table for **miserable**.

How would you feel if . . . ?

Think about the situation that is described below. Think about how you would feel if it happened to you. Then,

1   Make a list of words to describe your feelings. Use the word lists, but add any others that are suitable.
2   Use the words in a short piece of writing describing your feelings.

Your parents have promised that this year you can go on holiday with some friends, to a holiday centre on the coast. About a week before the holiday is due to begin, the holiday centre is flooded out and all holidays are cancelled.

Down in the mouth

A and B are friends, but they support opposing teams (you choose the sport and the names of the teams). A's team has just beaten B's team very easily. A and B meet afterwards and discuss the match and how they feel about it. Write the script of their conversation, using as many words as possible from the lists.

Acknowledgements

The publishers would like to thank the following for permission to reproduce photographs and other copyright material:

ActionAid p.56; **Adidas/Young and Rubicam Ltd.** p.41; **Aspect/David Higgs** p.50; **Barnaby's Picture Library** pp.90 (right), 91 (bottom); **BBC Hulton Picture Library** p.90 (left); **British Hovercraft Corporation** p.85 (bottom left); **Martin Chillmaid** pp.44–45 (all), 60 (all); **Lee Cooper/Camron P.R. Ltd.** p.41; **André Deutsch** p.68; **Elida/J. Walter Thompson Company Ltd.** p.4; **Granada Television** p.73; **Grattan plc** p.40; **Haymarket Publishing Ltd.** p.85 (bottom right); **Rob Judges** pp.6 (centre left), 7 (top right), 85 (top right), 100 (all), 106, 110 (both), 112–113 (all); **Le Clip S. A.** p.40; **Julia MacRae Books** p.69; **Mencap** p.56; **John Millar** pp.22, 24–25 (all), 43; **National Anti Vivisection Society** p.56; **O.I.S.E., Oxford** pp.108–109 (all); **Picturepoint** p.91 (top); **Renault UK/ McCormick – Publicis** pp.38–39; **Rex Features** p.85 (top left); **Timex** p.85 (bottom centre); **Tissot/Collett, Dickenson, Pearce and Partners Ltd.** p.40; **Topham Picture Library** p.91 (centre); **John Twinning** pp.6 (top, centre right, and bottom), 7 (centre left and right, bottom); **Careers Service, Worcester County Council** p.46.

The illustrations are by Judy Brown, Caroline Brunt, Kate Charlesworth, Helen Charlton, John Cooper, Gerard Gibson, Sue Heap, Chris Hill, Richard Hook, Oxford Illustrators, David Jackson, Conny Jude, Maggie Ling, Valerie Littlewood, Alan Marks, Chris Molan, Helen Parsley, Chris Price, Joanna Quinn, R D H Artists, Chris Riddell, Adrian Salmon, Nick Sharratt, and Stephen Wright.

We are grateful for permission to include the following copyright material: Ray Bradbury: from *The Playground*. Reprinted by permission of Abner Stein. John Branfield: from *Sugar Mouse* (1973). Reprinted by permission of Victor Gollancz Ltd. Paul Dehn: "Gutter Press" from *The Fern on the Rock* (Hamish Hamilton, 1965). Reprinted by permission of James Bernard, Literary Executor. Adrian Douglas: from *For Beauty Douglas*. Reprinted by permission of W H Allen Publishers. Jüri Gabriel: extract and table from *Unqualified Success* (Kestrel Books, 1984) pp.16–7, 23. Copyright © Jüri Gabriel, 1984. Reprinted by permission of Penguin Books Ltd. Susan Griffin: 'Three poems for women' from *In the Pink* (Women's Press, 1983). Nigel Hinton: from *Collision Course* (1983). Reprinted by permission of Oxford University Press. Janni Howker: from *Badger on the Barge* (Julia MacRae Books and Fontana Lions). Used with permission. Stella Ibekwe: 'Everybody Else Does It' from *More to Life than Mr Right*, ed. R. Stokes. Reprinted by permission of Piccadilly Press Ltd. Geraldine Kaye: 'Comfort Goes to Ghana' from *Comfort Herself* (1985). Reprinted by permission of André Deutsch. Penelope Lively: 'Princess by Mistake' from *Uninvited Ghosts* (1984). Reprinted by permission of William Heinemann Ltd. Adrian Mitchell: 'Back in the Playground Blues' from *For Beauty Douglas*. Reprinted by permission of W. H. Allen & Co plc. R K Narayan: 'The Evening Gift' from *Under the Banyan Tree* (1985). Reprinted by permission of William Heinemann Ltd. Jan Needle: from *Going Out* (Collins, 1982). Gareth Owen: "Typewriter Class" from *Song of the City*. Copyright © Gareth Owen 1985. Reprinted by permission of William Collins Sons & Co Ltd. *Oxford Senior Dictionary* (1982): entries reproduced by permission of Oxford University Press. Denys Parsons (ed.): extract from *Funny Ha Ha and Funny Peculiar* published by Pan Books Ltd., used with permission. Karen Payne: 'Advice to a Daughter' from *Between Ourselves* edited by Karen Payne (1983). Reprinted by permission of Michael Joseph Ltd. Laurie Taylor: from *In the Underworld* (1984). Reprinted by permission of Basil Blackwell Publisher.

Although every effort has been made to trace and contact copyright holders before publication we have not always been successful. If notified the publishers will be pleased to rectify any errors or omissions at the earliest opportunity.